THE BEDROOM SUPER PRODUCER

THE BEDROOM SUPER PRODUCER

Take the secret oath. Join an elite order of composers. Quit your nine-to-five, and earn six figures.

J. T. CLOUTIER

Copyright © 2017 J. T. Cloutier
All rights reserved.

ISBN-13: 9781537658063
ISBN-10: 1537658069

Contents

Acknowledgments: · xi
Introduction: How I Quit a Six-Figure Job at a
              Fortune 500 Company with No Hesitation
              Whatsoever · xiii
                  Choosing Plan B · xiv
                  This Part of My Life Is Called Depression · · · xvi
                  What You Will Learn · · · · · · · · · · · · · · · · · xvii
                  What You Will *Not* Learn · · · · · · · · · · · · · · · xix

Chapter 1 Darwin's Law: Only the Strong Survive · · · · · · · · · · 1
          Our Secret Oath · 2
Chapter 2 Becoming an Entrepreneur: Changing One's Mentality
          from Artistic Creator to Business-Value Creator · · · · · · 4
          Leases versus Exclusive Licenses · · · · · · · · · · · · · 4
Chapter 3 Finding a Marketplace: Understanding the Numbers
          Game · 7
          Content Is King · 7
          Let Me Google That for You · · · · · · · · · · · · · · 9
          Finding a Home for Your Music · · · · · · · · · · · · 9
          Musiclibraryreport.com · · · · · · · · · · · · · · · · · 9
          To Be Exclusive or Not to Be · · · · · · · · · · · · · 11

	PROs	12
	Tell it like it is, J. T.	13
Chapter 4	Creating a Product That Sells: Setting Your Music Apart without Compromising Sales Potential	14
	Finding a Niche	14
	Do Your Homework	15
	The Sausage Factory	16
	Examine the Competition (but Not Too Much)	16
	Create Meaningful Relationships	17
Chapter 5	What Is a Bedroom Super Producer?: Understanding the Math behind the Book's Claim	18
	Products versus Services	19
	Let's Do the Math	19
Chapter 6	A Method to the Madness: Becoming the Usain Bolt of Music Production	22
	Time Is Money	22
	Self-Teaching	23
	This Is Still Music, Ya Know	24
	Tools of a Master Craftsman	25
	Native Instruments	27
	8DIO	27
	Output Sounds	27
	Project Sam	27
	Sonokinetic	28
	Heavyocity	28
	Spitfire Audio	28
	A Sound Librarian You Will Be	28
	Four Key Steps to Becoming a Sound Librarian	29
	Step 1: Buy Your Libraries	29
	Step 2: Create a Classification Method	30
	Step 3: Active HD versus Archive HD	33

Step 4: Experiment with Depth and Width	33
The Brain of the Operation	34
Arrange Window	35
Piano Roll	35
Mixer	35
Templates and Presets	35
Song Templates	35
Mixing and Mastering Presets	37
Mixing Channel Strips	37
Mastering Effect Chains	38
VST Presets	40
Mix as You Go	40
Timbre	41
Texture	41
Dynamics	42
Rhythm	42
Melody	42
Harmony	43
Form	43
Actual Mixing	43
Song Classification System	44
Song-Naming Convention	44
Song Folder Nomenclature	45
It's Like Managing an Airport	46
To-Dos	48
Chapter 7 Sound Fundamentals: Writing Music That Moves People	50
Beginners	51
Intermediate	51
Experts	51
Chord Progressions	52

	I V VI IV	52
	Scales and Modes	53
	Melodies	53
	Anthem	54
	Minimalistic	54
	Rhythm and Groove	55
	Chordbot	55
	EZKeys	56
	Tones, Textures, and Form	57
	Layering	57
	Lessons learned	58
Chapter 8	Pop but Not Pop: Formatting Your Music for Media	60
	The Edits Game	60
	Full Song	62
	Sixty Seconds	63
	Thirty Seconds	64
	Fifteen Seconds	65
	Stinger	66
	Loops	67
	Loops Tips	67
	Lessons learned	67
Chapter 9	Inspire the Creatives: Becoming Your Own Personal Marketing Guru	69
	Song Titles	70
	Song Descriptions	71
	Metadata	72
	Genre(s)	72
	Mood(s)	72
	Instrument(s)	72
	Tag(s)	72
	Easier Said Than Done	73

Pricing · 73
Lessons learned · 74
Chapter 10 Beyond Stock Music: Multiple Streams of
Musical Income · 76
  A Strong Presence and Brand · · · · · · · · · · · 76
  A Timeless Logo · · · · · · · · · · · · · · · · · · · 77
  Simplicity · 77
  Memorability · 77
  Endurance · 77
  Versatility · 78
  Appropriateness · · · · · · · · · · · · · · · · · · · 78
  A Strong Brand · 78
  Define Your Personality · · · · · · · · · · · · · · 78
  Define Your Vision · · · · · · · · · · · · · · · · · · 79
  Communicate with Personality and Confidence · · · 79
  Your Own.com · 79
  The Money Is in the List · · · · · · · · · · · · · · 80
  The Social Network · · · · · · · · · · · · · · · · · 81
  Milking the Creative Cow · · · · · · · · · · · · · 83
  Drum Kits · 83
  Synth Presets · 84
  Kontakt Libraries · · · · · · · · · · · · · · · · · · · 85
  Templates · 86
  Premium Video Courses · · · · · · · · · · · · · · 86
  The Placement Game · · · · · · · · · · · · · · · · 87
Chapter 11 Composer Self-Help: Creating a Lifestyle That Will
Help You Thrive · · · · · · · · · · · · · · · · · · · 89
  The Seven Pillars · · · · · · · · · · · · · · · · · · · 90
  Nutrition · 91
  Exercise · 91
  Take Out the Trash · · · · · · · · · · · · · · · · · · 93

Meditation · 94
Reading · 94
Love Thyself · 94
Sleep · 95
Relationships · 96
Keep Learning · 97
Invest in Experiences, Not Things · · · · · · · · · · · 98
Well, then, what the fuck does? · · · · · · · · · · · · · 99

Conclusion

Why, oh, why didn't i take the blue pill?: Let
yourself see just how deep the rabbit hole goes · · ·100
A Business Plan ·101
A Paradigm Shift ·101
Mental Tools ·101
Work Tools ·102
A Proven Musical Approach · · · · · · · · · · · · · ·102
Marketing Tactics ·102
Branding Tactics ·102
Multiple Streams of Income · · · · · · · · · · · · · ·102
A Framework for Producer Happiness · · · · · · · ·103

Acknowledgments

This book is dedicated to the following:

My parents for letting me drop the bass and paying for my college education (even if in the long run I didn't choose *plan B*) and for letting me tweak kick drums for hours without even complaining about the bass.

My brother, Louis, for making me a businessman and for having this endless conversation about the possibility of making it as a musician over and over and over again (until my vision was completed in my head).

My best friend, BK, who put the universe's wheels in motion by showing me the secret ways of the bedroom super producers.

My cousin Tony for being there from day one and being the most innovative beat mind there is.

My friend D-Low for hustling my first beat tapes everywhere across town and for rap-proofing every single one of my beats.

My ex-wife, Anaïs, for always believing in my dream—you stayed by my side through depression and dark times, and for that I have the utmost respect.

My ex-girlfriend Antonine for encouraging me to quit my high-salary corporate job and for sharing my first year as a bedroom super producer—stressful times.

My long-time friend 2Faces for showing me the ropes of the music-production world—I remember to this day how you taught me to pick the drum sounds to create a cohesive kit.

All of my awesome friends and family.

All of my haters—you help me get better every day.

Introduction

How I Quit a Six-Figure Job at a Fortune 500 Company with No Hesitation Whatsoever

Life has this unrelenting way of kicking you in the nuts (ladies, pardon my choice of words, but you know what I mean), especially when you are not living your life's true purpose.

This book is a testament to the fact that dreams do come true. All of that wishy-washy, self-help stuff about believing in one's self and the law of attraction actually works—big time.

I have been preaching what is between these pages for quite some time now. Some fellow composers have listened and created a substantial income for themselves. Some did not listen and are still clueless. This is powerful stuff. It took me a lifetime of mistakes to create a formula that works consistently. I shall now pass it on to others who want to live meaningful lives, earning a living through their artistic passion—people who have the sack to endure being kicked in the groin several times and ask for more (shout out to Gary Vee) because they know that the only way to live is by following their lifelong dreams.

Choosing Plan B

Twenty years ago, I had no idea what kind of journey I was about to embark on when I sat down in front of the computer to make my first beat. That was in 1996, the year Tupac Shakur released *All Eyez on Me*, the Fugees released *The Score*, and Jay-Z released *Reasonable Doubt*. We were witnessing what some call the golden era of hip-hop. The revolution was televised—live and unadulterated.

For white Canadian suburban kids like me, this culture was like crack. We watched hip-hop movies, read hip-hop magazines, listened to hip-hop records, and dressed in baggy clothes. Personally, my fascination stemmed from the beats: the thick, funky bass lines, the hard drums, and the MC's tight flow. I became obsessed with the musical aspect of hip-hop and had to learn everything there was to learn about making beats.

Back then, there was no Internet (figuratively speaking, of course). You could not download albums, songs, music software, or VSTs. In order to make rap beats, you pretty much had to figure everything out on your own. This constraint planted the seed of self-teaching in me, and to this day, it helps me evolve as a composer instead of getting stuck in a certain space and time (becoming an autodidact is going to be very important down the line, so keep this in mind).

One day, a geek friend of mine in high school showed me this ugly DOS program that allowed a person to record sounds in the computer, play them on the keyboard like on a piano, and sequence them into patterns and songs. He was making this experimental brand of acid house, but I knew exactly what I would use it for. The program was called Impulse Tracker, the archaic ancestor of FL Studio.

I started to dedicate all my evenings and weekends to learning how to sample open drums, funk loops, and soul intros from CDs to record what I called "delicates" on cassette tapes. When it was sunny outside and my friends were playing basketball, I stayed inside and made beats. When it was time to study for a math exam, I waited until the very last minute because, well, beats came first. When my mom called us for supper, I ate alone because I had to finish some beat. Some kids cry when their parents confiscate their gaming console. Mine had to threaten me to take away the music gear in order for me to do my regular chores.

When high school came to an end, I started to have these talks with my folks about choosing a career path. Because music had always been just a hobby (and my parents made sure it stayed that way), it never occurred to me to see it as a potential career. Instead, I chose plan B. I was a good momma's boy and got a college degree in graphic design. Then I got a master's degree and worked a slew of stable but boring web-design jobs. Life wasn't very hard, but it was far from fulfilling.

I like graphic design. A lot. But I *love* music. The first is like a fun little game I'm pretty good at; the latter is a grand love story (yes, that much). This obsession drove me to work nights and weekends (that's after forty-plus hours behind a desk) for the next fifteen years in the hopes that one day I would be able to pay the bills by doing the one thing I loved the most in this world: composing music. I knew that if I could achieve this one goal, I would find satisfaction. Hell, I'm going to say it: I would have a real shot at happiness. So for fifteen years, I paid the bills with one job while building a side business. It took all of my time and energy.

The tough part was having this virus grow inside of me, this unshakable feeling that something was never quite right. It slyly started with a few hits of the snooze button. Then the morning showers got longer. Before long, the simple idea of going to work became nauseating. I spent eight hours a day watching the clock tick, hoping the hours were magically going to vanish so I could go back home and make music.

When I finally got there, I was exhausted. There was no more energy left in the tank. On some nights, I felt good enough, but my girlfriend reminded me that I agreed to have dinner with her parents a month ago. Soon, I started to see everything as an obstacle in my path, blocking me from getting enough time to work on my craft and become the super producer I always knew lay dormant inside of me. I became aggressive and antisocial. I tried to switch jobs, get pay raises, take more vacations, anything to give me a little motivation boost, but the feeling simply did not go away.

This Part of My Life Is Called Depression

I had to go through divorce, lose a home, see my newborn son only once every two weeks, and do two full years of psychotherapy before coming to the difficult realization that something had to change.

Something had become very fucked up along the way, and I had to fix it—now. This something was me. I had to change my perception of myself. A mentor of mine once said to lose the internal loser talk. I did. And like the mythical phoenix, I rose from the ashes and built myself anew. When you feel like you lost everything, you have two options: drown in self-pity or go to war. I chose to take arms and fight with everything I had left.

Fast-forward through two years of binge drinking and other self-destructive patterns, and I had lost thirty pounds and felt younger than ever. I was head of the user-experience department in a Fortune 500 company. I was earning a six-figure salary, wearing fancy suits to work, and driving a brand-new car, and I had a beautiful new girlfriend. I had made it. Or so I thought.

The honeymoon rapidly faded away. In a matter of a few months, I was back to square one, hating my job and clueless about what it took to make me happy. And then it dawned on me. It wasn't about the money. It wasn't about the social status and recognition. It was about freedom. It wasn't about waiting for it to happen; it was about making it happen by all means necessary.

On that fateful morning of November 2013, I pulled the trigger (figuratively speaking—come on now). I did myself a great favor and fired myself from the corporation. I threw away what my poor mom thought was a perfect life for me. I never looked back. Today, I earn more money, work fewer hours than ever before, and feel like I am truly happy. True story.

What You Will Learn

If you are reading this book, I assume you are a bedroom music producer and you want to take your game to the next level. You want to be part of the elite and become a "bedroom super producer" (BSP). But JT…Who are these highly secretive people you call BSPs, and what is their secret sauce? Good question! BSPs take many shapes and forms, but we have common traits:

- We are regular women and men.
- We live everywhere around the world.

- We usually work from home, just like you.
- We are very passionate about music, marketing, and business.
- We understand every aspect of the music-licensing game.
- We are business-minded individuals.
- We monetize every hour spent in front of the computer.
- We design our lifestyle to attain happiness as well as business success.
- We live off beats.

Here is the main difference: bedroom super producers build sustainable, automated incomes from their musical activities. Better yet, their methods optimize their wages to make them comparable to some of the best-known music super producers in the world, without having to live with the pressure of the limelight.

This book will teach you how to make this transition. Here are some of the steps you will learn to make this happen:

- How to change your mental state to make the crucial leap from artist to creative entrepreneur
- How to find sales partners who will do all the dirty work for you (marketing, driving traffic, programming, and so on)
- How to craft a musical product that sells
- How to maximize your productivity and efficiency to work at an hourly rate that rivals those of your favorite super producers
- How to drive even more traffic to your songs by mastering marketing copy and keyword strategies
- How to monetize every second you spend in front of your equipment, creating sounds, melodies, and production tools
- How to create habits that sustain lifelong creativity

What You Will *Not* Learn

I can show you the pond, show you how to build a fishing cane, and show you how to actually fish, but I cannot create the hunger you will need to go fishing day after day.

Only your life experience will build the mental trigger that you need in order to have the courage, dedication, and incredible resilience to walk the way of the bedroom super producer.

CHAPTER 1

DARWIN'S LAW

ONLY THE STRONG SURVIVE

Trust me when I say this: what you will learn in this book takes hard work. Repeat after me: hard work.

Just like you, I have been looking for shortcuts and get-rich-quick schemes. There are none as far as I know (what a cliché). On the flip side, what I offer here is a sound business model that will create a steady stream of automated income.

Creating products that can be sold online to generate an automated stream of income is the future. The richest people in the world will all tell you the same thing: it takes multiple streams of (ideally automated) income to achieve true financial freedom. I humbly offer you one method to build a stream that is in line with your passion for music.

Oh…you are still here? Are you ready to work hard? Relentlessly? Are you humble and patient enough to listen and learn? Good. Let's go to work.

But before I lay before you the (major) keys to success, you will have to pledge allegiance to the secret order of bedroom super producers by repeating out loud the following ten commandments.

Our Secret Oath

Commandment 1
I shall be patient.

Commandment 2
I shall not dwell in self-doubt.

Commandment 3
I shall work on my craft every day, notwithstanding inspiration.

Commandment 4
I shall always find ways to improve my sound, technique, and musical knowledge.

Commandment 5
I shall improve in all areas of my life, as my creativity is but a reflection of my inner well-being.

Commandment 6
I shall find mentorship.

Commandment 7
I shall find partnership.

Commandment 8
I shall not covet my neighbor's achievements (remember what Jay-Z said about jealousy).

Commandment 9
I shall never give up.

Commandment 10
I shall seek to make insane bangers every step of the way.

Welcome, sisters and brothers. You are now members of a very elite secret society. Not respecting the oath you have just taken could have dire consequences on your life and your life only. Do not waste the precious gift bestowed upon you: your limitless talent and creativity.

CHAPTER 2

BECOMING AN ENTREPRENEUR
CHANGING ONE'S MENTALITY FROM ARTISTIC CREATOR TO BUSINESS-VALUE CREATOR

We are artists. We are also parents. Each of our beats is our precious baby. As parents, it's always difficult to let one go, especially if the adoptive parents (read rappers and singers) seem unworthy. Let's destroy this paradigm right now because this is what stops most bedroom producers from going from hobbyists to business owners.

Rule 1
Beats are digital products, not babies.

Leases versus Exclusive Licenses

Leases, or nonexclusive licenses, are rights of usage sold by a composer to a customer, allowing that customer to use a song within a defined context (audience size, media channel type, and so on). The term "nonexclusive" refers to the fact that the customer will not be the sole proprietor of the license, allowing the composer to sell usage rights for the song to as many customers as she or he pleases.

Exclusive licenses should therefore be priced accordingly, as they limit a song to only one customer.

As artists, we are naturally drawn to putting the highest possible price tags on our preferred works of art. This way of thinking puts us in the first beat-selling category: high-priced exclusive licenses sold to only one customer. From a business standpoint, this is a flawed approach as it greatly reduces the number of potential returning customers.

Rule 2
Beats are to be sold at low prices (nonexclusive licenses) to as many customers as possible.

The pioneers of Soundclick.com understood the nonexclusive license model a long time ago. While selling low-priced, nonexclusive licenses on your own website is a very viable business model, it's limited by your budget to compete in the high-stakes paid-traffic game. I assume you are just starting out. If that's the case, you have approximately zero dollars to invest in paid traffic and advertising, while your competition has thousands, if not millions. If you want to move quickly (and I bet you do), you will have to find one or several marketplaces. A marketplace is a website that will automate your music sales to its high volume of returning customers.

Rule 3
Use a marketplace's high traffic to maximize the size of your audience and automate your nonexclusive music license sales.

Some people will tell you that entrepreneurs are born, not bred. I disagree. The first step is to accept the aforementioned rules of the game. The second step is to enter the ring and compete. The third and last step is to never give up. If you complete these steps on a daily basis, congratulations: you now have the mental habits of an entrepreneur. Rinse and repeat.

CHAPTER 3
FINDING A MARKETPLACE
UNDERSTANDING THE NUMBERS GAME

By now, you are no longer limited by your artist mentality, and you have accepted seeing yourself as a business owner. You understand that your craft is to be sold at lower prices but at a much higher volume.

You may still have doubts as to why choosing a marketplace is a far better business strategy at this stage rather than creating your own beat-selling website. First of all, you want to make music, not become a marketing guru, right? Second, the answer lies in the marketplace's type of customers and their sheer number. Let me explain.

Content Is King
If you study online marketing, you have heard this catch phrase countless times. Ladies and gentlemen, let me drop a little Internet knowledge gem on y'all: traffic goes wherever quality content is found. Moreover, never in the history of humankind has the need for content been so great.

The web ecosystem is made up of two main actors: content consumers and content creators. Newsflash: we are content creators. And we now work for content creators.

Rule 4
Content is king. Content creators need music. Marketplaces sell music to content creators.

Here are a few examples of content creators that we are now working for:

- Businesses producing corporate videos
- Freelance cinematographers producing corporate videos and TV ads for businesses
- Professional bloggers
- YouTubers
- Motion graphics firms
- Hobbyists who do not want their content removed from YouTube

Catch my drift? Content creators are any person or business entity who need music to enhance the quality of their content. Let me tell you something else: these people *need* your music more than ever. They are more numerous than artists looking for beats, and they are more serious in their business endeavors. For them, it's not just about a mixtape dropping soon; it's about growing their topline revenue.

Rule 5
Content creation is a necessity for the new digital economy. Content creators are more numerous than artists. Content creators are more serious, paying, and returning customers.

Let Me Google That for You

Open your browser to google.com and type in any combination of the following keywords:

- Stock music
- Royalty-free music
- Music library
- Music for media
- Production music
- Music licensing

Spoiler alert: by doing so, you will find hundreds, if not thousands, of websites ready to sell your product now. These are the marketplaces I was referring to earlier. For some of you, it's the first time you've ever heard of stock music or royalty-free music marketplaces. Now that this world of opportunity has been unveiled to you, let me show you how deep the rabbit hole goes.

Finding a Home for Your Music
Musiclibraryreport.com

This website is your new best friend. It is the strongest community of music composers discussing and rating the web's best music marketplaces (or libraries) on a daily basis. It has free content, but I highly recommend getting a paid membership to be able to take part in the forum discussions, read all blogs and user comments, and so on.

Start with a one-month subscription, and visit the website every day to find music libraries that cater to your musical style while offering contracts that fit your business model. This search is extremely important.

Beyond music library ratings and discussions, you will also find a wealth of tips and tricks about how to submit music, licensing models, contract types, and the like. You will literally find everything a media composer (that's what we are called in relation to content creators) should know before entering the highly competitive world of music licensing.

When searching for your main music library, you will see patterns emerge:

- Big libraries with tens of thousands of songs usually offer nonexclusive deals.
- Nonexclusive libraries have more composers onboard (more competition).
- Nonexclusive contracts offer smaller payouts.
- Exclusive boutique libraries have fewer composers and less music but offer bigger payouts.
- Boutique libraries are tougher to sign with, especially if you are a beginner.
- Big libraries get more traffic.
- Big libraries have more rubbish music and make your music harder to find.

All music libraries come with their fair share of advantages and disadvantages. When looking for a home to your music, strike a balance: large enough traffic, quality music-browsing experience, quality music, decent payout policy, fair contracts, and so on.

Use musiclibraryreport.com to build a spreadsheet that will help you compare music libraries before signing one or several contracts.

To Be Exclusive or Not to Be

To work with a music library, you will have to sign a contract. There are two main types of agreements:

- Exclusive: the music you sell on their website cannot be sold elsewhere.
- Nonexclusive: the music you sell on their website can be sold elsewhere.

Some libraries will even tell you they cannot do business with you if you have signed a contract with some listed libraries. The competition is fierce. But the good news is they need you.

Because you are limited in the number of songs you can produce each week, month, or year, be careful where you lay your eggs. Signing one exclusive contract can work, but if the library doesn't sell or place your work, that music is trapped (depending on the duration of the contract).

Signing multiple nonexclusive deals can also work, but it can rapidly become a song uploading and labeling nightmare. Again, strike a balance. A great way to start is to sign one exclusive deal and two nonexclusive ones. Send 50 percent of your work each way. After a year, you can evaluate who moves more of your product (ah, the good ol' drug-dealer slang). That way, you can focus on the libraries that work best for you.

Once you have chosen your libraries, it's time to submit songs for approval. Always put your best work first. If you are a hip-hop producer, do not submit pop-rock songs. The key is to get in. You will not have a second chance to make a great first impression.

When your work is deemed to be of good enough quality, get your contract reviewed by a lawyer. Have her or him help you understand the duration, limits, ownership details, and payout policy. Ever heard of artists getting ripped off by music labels? Not reading the contract leads to horror stories of that sort.

PROs

Ever heard of PROs? It's an acronym for music *performance rights organization*. Ever heard the acronyms ASCAP or BMI? Those are the main PROs in the United States.

When signing contracts with libraries, you're hiring them as your music publisher. Music publishers help you get your music sold and placed for public usage (TV, radio, Internet, and the like). They also handle the paperwork when your music is used. This generates money for the both of you, so the publisher needs the composer to have a PRO member number. After PROs have monitored song usage, they are able to distribute money based on play counts.

Rule of thumb: even if the library you sign with does not need your PRO membership number, get one. You will need it in the future, and you don't want to get it too late.

I once had a number-one song playing on the most-listened-to rush-hour radio show in my hometown, and I only registered with a PRO a year later. I left thousands of dollars on the table because my PRO could only make retroactive payments for a period of six months. That money was mine and mine alone. Becoming a PRO member is very cheap or even free in some cases. Do not procrastinate.

TELL IT LIKE IT IS, J. T.

Music for media might not appear to you as the most glamorous of music career branches. Maybe that's why very few composers I speak with know about it. The model I propose in this book has two core strengths:

1. It allows you to focus on making music, not marketing it.
2. It allows you to design your lifestyle with automated income from online music sales.

Now that, I'm sure, everyone can relate to. Finding the right stock-music marketplaces is by far the fastest route to achieving the aforementioned career goals. As I have said earlier, the number of potential customers and their relative seriousness is a definite advantage over other types of music marketplaces.

Get on musiclibraryreport.com. Take part in discussions. Ask questions to seasoned vets. Get legal help to understand your contracts. Make music. Make money.

CHAPTER 4
CREATING A PRODUCT THAT SELLS
SETTING YOUR MUSIC APART WITHOUT COMPROMISING SALES POTENTIAL

There is one catch to what this book sells: unless your product sounds world class and appeals to a large enough audience, forget about composing for media as your main source of income.

Fortunately for you, I know exactly how to get there.

Finding a Niche

To be competitive from the get-go, you need a niche. You need to compose music that libraries need but do not have in sufficient quantity or quality. Most importantly, you need to find a style that highlights your strengths and hides your weaknesses as a musician.

Find a music style in which you can compose effortlessly, day in and day out.

When I started out five years ago, I was mainly a hip-hop producer. The hip-hop songs used in media back then were these corny, funky-inspired, new-jack-swing types of songs (you know, the ones with tacky trumpet scratches). Big business was ready to sound hip.

I knew that because of the overwhelming success of hip-hop music worldwide, libraries would soon need a large amount of quality, *genuine*-sounding hip-hop. That's exactly how I positioned myself as a composer when I started to reach out to music libraries. While some libraries were not interested in pursuing hip-hop as a genre in their catalog, the ones that did made a very special place for me. That allowed me to get a lot of visibility early on and get sales going very quickly.

Do Your Homework

Now that you have found your niche, it's time to understand what kind of songs businesses actually buy in that genre. If you are an EDM producer, what kind of EDM-influenced tracks do you hear in fashion and beauty TV ads? What famous artist's track did such-and-such car company use for its latest Super Bowl spot?

The key is to understand your customers' tastes and needs. While you may want to go for a super edgy Skrillex-style dubstep sound, big companies may need to cater to a more family-oriented audience, and, therefore, a smoother and more uplifting Calvin Harris type of sound works best.

Pay attention. Every day, we are bombarded by YouTube, Facebook, and TV ads. While the rest of the world is pressing the skip button, we are now taking notes. Watching a movie or a TV series on Netflix? We are paying close attention to the music. We are dissecting the sounds, the arrangement, the tempo, the textures, the chords, and the melodies.

You need to understand why agencies and music supervisors chose certain songs. You need to learn from those choices and incorporate what you have learned into your niche.

Here's a very simple example. Heavily delayed pop-rock guitar music (à la U2) is a media mainstay. How would those guitars sound over an electronica/ambient track? Over an orchestral arrangement? Over a rap beat?

The Sausage Factory

You have a niche, and you have found a way to make this niche more accessible to a broader audience. Create five to ten tracks in that specific genre. Then let the market tell you if your hypothesis was right or wrong. Pay close attention to which track sells the most and try to understand why. Once you have done that, keep polishing your flagship type of track until you have two or three best sellers (read the next chapter to fully grasp what a best seller is in terms of numbers). Then create new niches. This process is endless.

Examine the Competition (but Not Too Much)

While focusing on your lane can increase your competitive advantage, you also need to be aware of what your fellow composers are doing and what works for them.

Fortunately for us, most libraries gather their best-selling items in listings ordered by musical style or context of usage (sports, drama, corporate, and so on). Take notes. Analyze these songs and understand why customers buy them again and again.

Also try to locate what the most popular musical genres are. Be careful: customers are somewhat lazy (aren't we all when it comes to browsing the web?). Most will not scroll to the fiftieth page of search results to find your hidden gem. They will buy their favorite song from the first page.

We want you on that first page.

Create Meaningful Relationships

Most of these libraries are actually very small companies where a handful of individuals do all the work. You want to make these people your allies. Once in a while, drop a short, courteous e-mail thanking them for their hard work and the opportunity they are giving you. After all, they are making your dream a reality.

Ask them what kinds of songs they will be needing and follow through with quality submissions. This is team work, and you want the libraries to notice your drive to make their business a success.

Do not bombard them with questions. You are an expert, and you are proactive. When songs are rejected, you can ask for a few pointers. Do not take rejection on a personal level. Move on quickly and sell that song elsewhere.

CHAPTER 5

WHAT IS A BEDROOM SUPER PRODUCER?

Understanding the Math behind the Book's Claim

The rules are simple. You must find one or several high-traffic websites to sell your broadcast-ready, original music. To go from bedroom producer to *bedroom super producer*, a crucial concept you will need to master is your hourly rate. We all know there is a finite number of hours in a day, and there is also a limited number of hours when we can be truly creative every day. We need to find ways to boost the hourly rate without wearing ourselves out.

Luckily for us, the digital economy truly has the potential to destroy the concepts of office face time and hourly rate as we know them. More importantly, it can help us break free of the rigid laws of salary growth (2 to 3 percent per year is not a raise, folks; it's inflation matching).

If you follow the rules in this book, not only will you be in full control of your salary raises, but you will also be able to work at an hourly rate you never had an idea was possible in the field of music production. The type of hourly rate I'm talking about is one that compares with those of your favorite production heroes. Real talk.

Products versus Services

As you may have noticed by now, I usually do not refer to music production as a service. Why? Because there is a big potential income difference between exchanging hours of services for money and selling production services packaged as products. The former is constrained by time; the latter is not. Products are only constrained by quality and value, parameters over which we have much more control. Once you understand this concept, your musical offering will never again be constrained by time. Instead, you will be on a mission to increase the number of products, their quality, and your overall efficiency to deliver them to market.

Let's Do the Math

Allow me to put my money where my mouth is. Let's start with a simple example.

Exclusive License Sale

You sell one exclusive license (one beat) for three hundred dollars.

You worked on this gem for eight to sixteen hours. Let's make this an average of twelve hours.

$300/12 hours = $25/hour

Not too bad. But can you sell one of those per week, consistently, for fifty weeks per year? It's harder than it sounds.

Let's apply the concept of productization.

You have put together a not-so-well-known beat website with traffic of roughly one hundred potential customers per day. Trust me, one hundred unique visitors per day can be quite a lot.

Let's apply the basic laws of web conversion to this one.

Nonexclusive Licenses on Your Own Beat-Selling Website
Web conversion average: let's work with 1 percent (this is what most e-commerce websites do).

Nonexclusive license cost: thirty dollars
Hours of work per beat: twelve hours
Yearly sales: one sale per beat per week (fifty weeks of business minus two weeks of vacation, the corporate average)

100 visitors × 1% = 1 buyer/day
1 sale × $30 × 50/12 hours = $125/hour

Wow, we have just multiplied our hourly rate by five. Can you name one local artist who buys beats for fifteen hundred dollars? I know I can't.

Driving and increasing traffic to a website is a complex process that takes a lot of time and expertise. It's doable, but, right now, you have purchased this book because you want to make money making music, not becoming a Google AdWords certified partner. Let's use the same nonexclusive license price tag, but let's crank up the traffic to the website ten times.

Nonexclusive Licenses on an Established Marketplace
Web conversion average: 1 percent

Nonexclusive license cost: thirty dollars
Hours of work per beat: twelve hours

1,000 visitors × 1% = 10 buyers/day
10 sales × $30 × 50/12 hours = $1,250/hour

Your beat has now earned you $15,000 in a year. That's major placement money right there.

Your hourly rate for this particular beat is a whopping $1,250 per hour. Catch my drift?

Ladies and gentlemen, this is how bedroom super producers are made. Trust me when I say this: these are real-life figures. I know of music-for-media superstars who make four to five times more (even ten is some isolated cases) on their best-selling songs. I have seen the sales reports.

These estimates could be more pessimistic or more aggressive. They do not account for less successful beats, but they also do not account for the fact that beats are sold over many years either. This is beside the point. The point is to understand this basic formula.

The Bedroom Super Producer Formula
Sell products, not services.
Make broadcast-sounding songs in fewer hours, every week.
Use marketplace traffic to generate multiple sales per day.
Measure your efficiency based on your new targeted hourly rate.
Consistently improve quality and speed.

Chapter 6

A Method to the Madness

Becoming the Usain Bolt of Music Production

Let's recap:

- You have switched your artist mentality to a business-friendly approach.
- You have researched music libraries and signed contracts.
- You have done your homework and found a niche that highlights your unique musical gift.
- You have a general idea of how to make that sound accessible to the masses.

Now let's get into the nitty-gritty. Let's make a science out of consistently creating music that sells to content creators around the world.

Time Is Money

This is your end of the stick. This is where you can make a big difference, consistently. I am referring to your speed and quality of execution. If you're going to make broadcast-ready songs (I'm talking about composed, mixed, and mastered in one, two, or maybe three working days), you're going to need every part of that machine well oiled.

Here are the main components of this machine:

- Self-teaching and continuous improvement
- Musicianship
- Use of the highest-quality sounds and libraries
- Intuitive sound classification system
- DAW mastery
- Song creation templates
- VST presets
- Mixing channel strips and presets
- Mastering presets
- Song classification system
- Song delivery system
- Task management and prioritization system

I know…those are a lot of things to worry about. Like with most productivity frameworks, let's tackle one item at a time. It will make the whole list easier to digest.

Self-Teaching

The ability to be self-taught is probably the most fundamental pillar of the bedroom super producer method. Choosing a career in music is accepting the fact that you will never know everything, let alone have the certainty that you know enough.

Because of this state of affairs, you will need a wealth of great teachers along the way who won't always be in your vicinity. Some are already dead, while some may live on the other side of an ocean.

That is why I advocate self-teaching, obviously using crucial learning material such as books, magazines, blogs, and video tutorials.

I have talked with a lot of fellow producers who claim that they cannot do it or that it's not their preferred way of learning things. I urge everyone to reconsider this position: you will not have enough time or money to sit in a classroom and pay someone to help you learn, hand in hand. Self-teaching plays a pivotal role in making you unique in unforeseeable ways, which, for a career in music, is a great advantage. Working in unorthodox ways does sometimes create benefits, whether it be new playing styles, recording techniques, or unusual harmonies.

Do the names Jimi Hendrix, Kurt Cobain, or David Bowie ring a bell for you? These legends had phenomenal careers, left us with timeless music and performances, *and* had no formal musical training. Yup…I know.

This Is Still Music, Ya Know

I will always remember the most important piece of advice Pharrell Williams once gave to aspiring producers during an interview: learn an instrument. While technology allows composers with no proper musical training to thrive in this industry, I side with Skateboard P on this one.

I recommend that you study musical theory and learn an instrument (piano or guitar), at least in your downtime. While learning an instrument is a fantastic way to improvise musical ideas as well as connect with your own music (there is something magical about hearing what your brain dictates to your fingers through a musical instrument), I suggest that you start with musical theory. The learning curve is less steep in my opinion, and at the end of the day, your customers connect primarily on an emotional level to the richness of your chord progressions and melodies.

If you have studied a little about marketing, you know that emotion drives purchasing behaviors (wink, wink). You can always enhance great musical ideas with more intricate playing styles later.

Depending on your preferred way of learning, there are fabulous books out there, but I highly recommend finding teachers on YouTube: it's free, and visual support will help you grasp the more complex notions. You should (will) spend a few hours every week improving your knowledge of scales, harmonies, melodies, modes, and rhythms.

Tools of a Master Craftsman

If you're a bassist or guitarist, it goes without saying that you will need ready-to-go instruments that stay in tune with quality pickups and fresh strings. As I am primarily a keyboardist, I will focus more on sound libraries as this is the way of the future in terms of achieving the biggest, most exciting, and best-recorded sound possible within the constraints of our method of production (broadcast-quality music recorded on time and budget, probably on a simple laptop).

At this stage, stock sounds and presets may not cut it anymore. You are in the big leagues. You need to use the best tools in order for your songs to be on par with the best. I will divide these sound-generation tools into two categories: software synthesizers and sampled instruments.

If your niche is electronic music, you will need the same soft synths that professionals use: FM8 and Massive for dubstep, Sylenth/Serum/Spire for house and EDM, and Zebra and Reaktor for ambient and experimental. There are also extremely useful romplers such as Nexus and Omnisphere with ready-to-go, great-sounding presets.

My point is not to create an exhaustive list of software synthesizers but to invite you to research the best tools for the desired style you want to produce as well as to develop a basic understanding of the strengths and weaknesses of each of these tools.

Try to concentrate your sound design efforts on two or three of these at the most. Your goal is to develop speed and efficiency. I highly suggest finding third-party companies who create preset patches for your go-to synthesizers. For now, you are not to become a world-class sound designer. Know your place in the food chain.

Over the years, I have always been looking for the most musical, colorful, and organic virtual instruments available. For speed, quality, and breadth of choice, I cannot emphasize enough the importance of developing a workflow focused primarily on sample libraries. Sample libraries are real-world instruments, as well as digital instruments, grouped on your MIDI keyboard through the use of a software sampler.

With the recent advances in processor performance, a composer can now have access to hundreds of sampled instruments right at his or her fingertips. The realism, musicality, and quality of sound of professional sample libraries nowadays are astounding.

I will always remember a conversation I had ten years ago with a fellow producer who was saying without a shadow of a doubt that computers would take over even the most intricate instruments such as orchestral strings and electric guitars. At the time, I thought it was nonsense. Today, 99 percent of listeners are fooled every day by sampled orchestras in movie trailers.

Composers can now effectively program fake ethnic guitars, string quartets, and concert grand pianos inside their laptops, unbeknownst to their customers, all thanks to the incredible power of modern software samplers.

In this category, the king of the hill is Kontakt by Native Instruments. You will need this tool, and you will have to know the best library developers. This will save you time, but, most importantly, it will also instantly bring a realism and richness to your compositions that are otherwise impossible to achieve without a big budget, a big studio, and expensive engineers and musicians.

Make no mistake: the music-for-media game is about world-class sounds. Fake-sounding strings do not cut it anymore. It needs to sound like the real deal. To get you started, I have assembled a short list of extremely professional, third-party library makers.

Native Instruments
A great starting point is buying Komplete, which is unbeatable in terms of value for the money. You get a wide array of industry-leading software synthesizers as well as incredible sample libraries for Kontakt.

8DIO
These guys changed my life. They make everything from the best orchestral scoring tools to edgy and current-sounding EDM libraries.

Output Sounds
A new player in the game, they have produced some of the most innovative libraries anyone has ever seen.

Project Sam
Symphobia is such a powerful tool if you want to add that big Hollywood sound without getting lost in all of the orchestra's instrument articulations.

Sonokinetic

Their orchestral phrase libraries can add a sense of realism that far surpasses any well-versed programmer's efforts.

Heavyocity

They are Native Instruments' partners; therefore, you get some of their best libraries as part of Komplete. They specialize in orchestral and trailer libraries. They also have some of the most organic-sounding percussion libraries out there.

Spitfire Audio

This British company offers some of the richest-sounding orchestral articulations as well as very original synth libraries for Kontakt. Let's not forget they are the makers of the incredible Hans Zimmer series.

This is just a short list of my personal favorites. A bedroom super producer should always be on the lookout for new and useful libraries. This is an ongoing process. Listen to YouTube demos. Download free demos and test them out.

Buy your libraries. This simple gesture goes a very long way as it allows developers to keep producing tools we can't work without, but, most importantly, it also unconsciously pushes you to dive deeper and master your libraries.

A Sound Librarian You Will Be

Bedroom super producers know their sound vault inside and out. They do not hesitate when it comes to finding that perfect 808. They know exactly where it resides on their hard drives. They also know where to look when a project calls for a 1950s-sounding snare recorded with a ribbon mic passed through a long spring reverb.

Collecting all kinds of sounds is easy. Putting time aside each week to fine-tune your classification methods takes hard work and dedication.

We want you to develop a mental map of your sound library. This map needs to be ingrained into your psyche in such a way that finding sounds on your hard drive no longer slows the creative process down. In fact, picking sounds is no longer a search property of your brain; it is now a simple recall function.

Geek talk aside, you need to have listened to each individual sample on your computer for that to happen. If the task seems impossible, it means you are still hoarding sounds. We want you out of that phase and on to the next one: frugality.

While having tons of sounds at your disposal may seem comforting at first, it will rapidly become a hurdle. In this digital age, it is very easy to have more sounds on a hard drive than is humanly possible to listen to in an entire lifetime. What good does this serve?

Four Key Steps to Becoming a Sound Librarian
Step 1: Buy Your Libraries

We have all been there. Downloading libraries illegally is easy and mainstream nowadays. How many YouTube tutorials have we seen with well-known DJs browsing through *tons* of torrent-named sound folders (for newbies, they are the ones with each word separated by commas)?

Now that you are making money with your music, not only is it unfair to sound designers worldwide, but it becomes very dangerous for you because your music is exposed to a much broader audience. If you are using libraries you have not paid for, you may get into legal troubles that your business may never recover from.

The other benefit of buying libraries is the creation of a heightened sense of curiosity, loyalty, and creativity. Investing money creates a real sense of ownership in your mind and in turn gives you far greater motivation to create something special using the library. Finally, the process of shopping and buying libraries limits the number of libraries you will be using. This is what we want: a quantity of options that your brain can actually process.

Step 2: Create a Classification Method

- By musical genre
- By instrument type
- By library type (Kontakt, WAVs single shots, loops, and so on)
- By song key (especially useful for melodic loops)
- By song tempo (most loop libraries are already set up this way)

Whichever method you choose needs to complement your production style. Do you start with chords and melodies? Drum beats? Cutting up loops?

I have been through dozens of such methods, and I'm still refining my process every day. Experiment.

Here is an overview of my classification method as it is right now:

Delicate Vault Architecture
> *Main go-to folders (preferred drum libraries and Kontakt instruments)*
>> *Instrument type (guitars, strings, and so on)*
>>> *Library type (Kontakt, Loops, and the rest)*
>>>> *Sound type (loop, single hit)*

Here is what it actually looks like with the drums folder open. Notice the width (number of folders on the first level of the HD) versus the depth (number of levels before actually previewing samples).

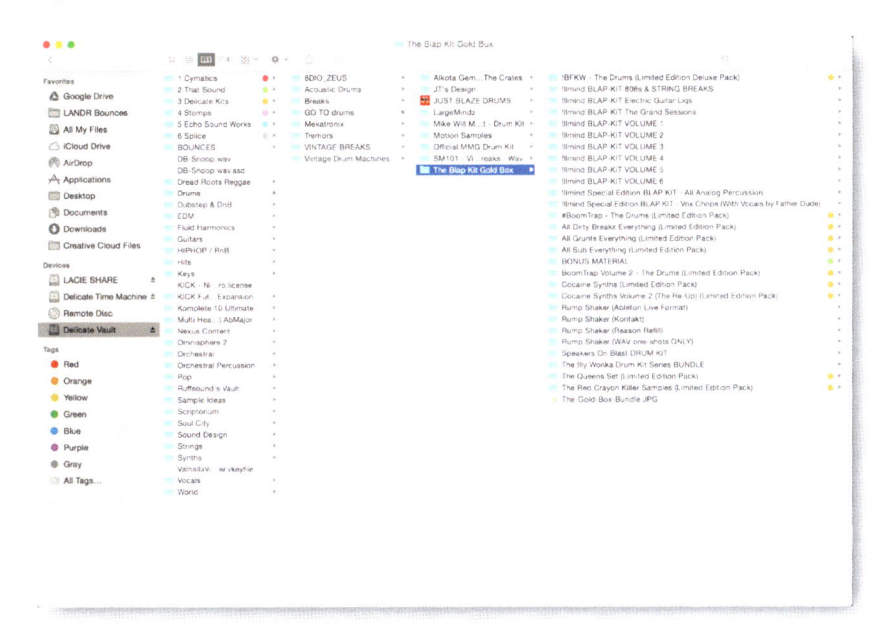

Fairly simple and straightforward, right?

Because I'm primarily an urban producer and usually start by crafting musical ideas on a piano, my method is hybridized so that drums and EDM folders appear on the same level as strings and keyboard libraries. My Kontakt browser displays my favorite piano library first: Alicia's Keys. I can then start putting drum and percussion tracks together using either That Sound or Cymatics libraries (notice the green and red dots at the very top).

That way, access to piano libraries is as quick as finding kicks and snares. My classification system, therefore, follows the way I work, not the other way around.

Quick Tip 1: Color Coding

A great way to help find your way through thousands of sounds labeled "Snare + Number.WAV" is to color code the files and folders. I use a traffic-light method for drum sounds:

- *Green is my favorite go-to sounds.*
- *Yellow is not bad but with restricted usage (sounds that have a narrower appeal in a specific genre).*
- *Red is experimental or unusable sounds (sometimes sound designers get a little too funky for my taste). Mental note: copy those sounds to an archive hard drive and delete them from the active one to reduce clutter.*

Quick Tip 2: Favoriting

Nowadays, a lot of plug-in developers have felt the producers' needs to accelerate workflow. Most of them include a way to classify and rate sounds and presets.

Rate your presets in Massive and other synths. Set up your Kontakt libraries by order of preference within the library browser. Rate Apple Loops in Logic.

Step 3: Active HD versus Archive HD

I am a very drastic person when it comes to digital file management. Some years ago, I deleted all sound files I had not bought with my own money (this is nothing to be proud of, but I have downloaded a few torrents in my days). That way, I cut a lot of junk libraries I had never even used and put focus on libraries I loved and worked with on a daily basis.

If you're not ready to flush down a lot of sounds you may not even use (or have not bought), here's what I suggest: use a main hard drive or a folder for the sounds you use on a regular basis, while archiving all other sounds to another hard drive, one that is ideally not connected to your work computer. Again, it's about creating an artificial urge to use key libraries while limiting the need to second-guess yourself and lose valuable time scrolling through thousands of average-sounding presets.

To create this secondary archive, I suggest using a rule such as the one we use when packing boxes before moving to a new home or apartment: if you haven't used it in the last year (I would even go as far as the last month), it has to go. The goal of this operation is to reduce mental clutter.

You want your brain to see and map out only the important files and folders. It can be scary at first as most producers tend to hoard at least a little, but in the long run, you will forget about those sounds you never really used in the first place.

Step 4: Experiment with Depth and Width

Depth and width are concepts I mastered in my previous life when I worked as a web content specialist. Back in those days, web pages needed to be accessible from the homepage using the lowest number of mouse clicks, forcing us to produce the most intuitive content architecture possible.

Because a web page had limited-screen real estate available for menus, we had to make sure the most important subjects/topics/sections were clickable at the highest level, while making sure important content did not get drowned in the said architecture.

- Wide content architecture: numerous entries on the first level with limited depth
- Deep content architecture: few entries on the first level with great content depth for each entry

My point is this: once your open your sound vault, you do not want to overwhelm your eyes with a bunch of folders you open just twice a year (creating an architecture that is too wide), but at the same time you do not want to dig super deep every time you need your favorite dub airhorn sample (too deep).

Refine your content architecture as often as possible. Make it easy to search through, ya dig?

The Brain of the Operation

A lot of beginners ask me this question: What is the best DAW (digital audio workstation)? This age-old question has a simple answer: the one that provides you with the quickest workflow.

In the digital age, all DAWs were pretty much created equal in terms of sonic quality. What you should look out for, then, is a user interface that makes it easy for you to create music. To choose the perfect DAW, you will need to understand three basic concepts: the arrange window, the piano roll, and the mixer.

Arrange Window

This is the graphical representation of a song's tracks. As the name implies, this window allows the bedroom super producer to arrange loops, sound hits, and MIDI information into a song with buildups, drops, choruses, breakdowns, and so on.

Piano Roll

This is where you record and edit MIDI information (chords, melodies, and drum beats).

Mixer

This is where you balance the levels and panning, add effects, and shape your musical idea into a broadcast-sounding gem.

All DAWs pretty much have them. Once you understand these three concepts, you are ready to test-drive any DAW out there. Download three demos and make a beat with each. Only then will you be able to tell which DAW provided you with the best workflow. Efficiency ain't nuthin' to mess wit'!

Now that you have chosen your weapon of choice, it's time to get to know it like the back of your hand. Learn the keyboard shortcuts. Watch tutorials to learn mixing and audio editing tricks. As I have mentioned earlier, technology can't slow you down when inspiration strikes.

Templates and Presets
Song Templates

This concept goes hand in hand with DAW mastery. When creating a new session, your DAW should automatically allow you to choose from a wide array of purpose-specific session templates.

Here are a few of mine:

- Basic session: 4/4, 120 bpm, four to eight tracks of both audio and MIDI tracks
- Orchestral trailer: 3/4 or 4/4, 135 bpm, orchestral instrument articulations loaded such as staccato strings, legato strings, staccato brass ensemble, legato horns, legato trumpets, timpani hits and rolls, boomers, impacts, and cymbals
- EDM: 4/4, 128 bpm, four-to-the-floor kick for sidechain compression, a selection of your favorite soft synths, and a Battery patch with your favorite kick samples
- Trap/hip-hop: 4/4, 70 to 80 bpm, your favorite 808 samples, two or three drum kits with kicks, snares, and high hats, three or four soft synths, and three or four sampler tracks

To create useful templates, try to choose repetitive tasks when making beats. These tasks will become the foundational elements of each of your song templates. The goal is to stop making the same actions over and over again. Cut library and plug-in load times in half.

Because you are also an apprentice sound librarian, you should take the classification a step further by creating go-to drum kits and sample collections. Two great plug-ins to create these are Native Instruments' Battery and Kontakt (Drum Rack in Ableton Live is pretty cool too). These two samplers are extremely powerful tools to create sound collections readily available at your fingertips through any MIDI controller.

Here are a few examples:

- Kicks: load your favorite twenty to thirty kicks all on one sampler patch
- Snares: same as kicks (ten boom bap snares, ten trap snares, ten EDM snares)

- Transition effects: ten risers, ten boomers, ten impacts (ideally cut on grid to allow easy time-stretching)

We all have a collection of sounds we are drawn to during most of our sessions. They sit perfectly in any mix and are always inspiring. Let's embrace this fact. Make access to these sounds lightning quick. How many times did Timbo and Pharrell use the same snare sound? There is a reason for that.

Mixing and Mastering Presets

Let's take the song template concept a step further and introduce the idea of mixing and mastering presets.

Mixing Channel Strips

Some purists will say, "This is impossible to automate; every mix is completely different." Let's agree to disagree for the sake of my example.

A bedroom super producer should have a wide array of go-to mixing-effect chains ready to be locked and loaded whenever an ongoing mix is not gelling or simply to speed up the process of loading individual effect plug-ins in the mixer.

Here are some basic mixing channel strips I use every day:

- EQ-Comp: I probably use this on 99.9 percent of my tracks. I use the equalizer for its tone-shaping abilities and compress the sound afterward just to keep control of the sound post-EQ. Why, then, should I load these plug-ins individually on each of my tracks when I can create new tracks and have them loaded automatically?

busses: I usually work with three different room sizes: [a short room], one long plate reverb and one large hall. [This gives] me enough options to separate my tracks spatially. When I open a new session, I already have these reverbs ready to start separating my sounds.
- Keyboard channel strips: Sampled keyboards can sound very stale out of the box. I like to put guitar amps, delays, reverbs, and tremolo on analog synths and electric pianos to mimic recordings of the '70s and '80s.
- Reverb-Comp: This is another great trick to breathe life into keyboard tracks. Put a long tail reverb first and use the compressor to duck (side chain) the sound using another sound as the trigger. Extreme compressor settings can put forward awesome grain and textures your ears didn't even know were there.

Quick Tip: If You Used It, Save It

As soon as you find an effect chain you like, name it and save it. Avoid using colorful commentary-type names such as "The last 808 ever" or "Some snare smack." Instead, detail the sound specifics: "Aggressive snare EQ+Comp+1/8 delay."

Mastering Effect Chains

Based on the musical genre of the song, you will develop a set of compression thresholds, EQ curves, and multiband compression and limiter values. You can start with something as simple as an Izotope Ozone preset. I think subtle mastering actually helps your mixing by letting you know if the kick is too loud or if the mids are shy.

I usually start with a mastering chain on which all plug-ins are set to the default value. Once my arrangement and mix start to resemble the final product, I will add 1 or 2 dB of compression to catch peaks and use my EQ to match the curve of a professional recording in the same genre/vibe as my composition. I use Fabfilter's ProQ2 to analyze and correct my master's frequencies. This arbitrary process helps me identify problem areas in my mix that I may not hear.

I have a tendency to leave in super-high (unwanted) frequencies above 15 kHz and to attenuate high mids (1 to 6 kHz) a little too much (voice frequencies) while composing/arranging. This process helps me compensate and fix these problem areas.

Again, the idea is to have a finished product by the end of the session, and I prefer to fix my song along the way instead of being left with an unmixable arrangement at the very end.

When my mix has attained satisfactory results, I apply 2 or 3 dB of limiting. You don't want to crush the mix, but limiting is essential to tell you if the drums need more compression, if your EDM kick is too loud, or if you could nudge a bit more bass in there.

My rule of thumb is this: if I can't match the levels of a similar professional recording, my mix needs fixing. You want to sit in the mastering engineer's chair for a minute in order to find insights into how good your mix really is. Unless you are a very seasoned mixing vet, only a quick mastering will highlight these problem areas.

If mastering is still voodoo to you, don't worry. Simply pass your mix through LANDR. This online drag-and-drop mastering service is a great mixing aid. I myself do the double whammy: I do a first master-as-I-go pass and finish it up in LANDR. That way, even though I don't have three or four sets of speakers, I know my final song will sound great in monitors, earphones, and car sound systems.

VST Presets

We now have a set of tools for the technical foundation of our song-making process. Now let's speed up the creative process. I asked you to define two or three software synthesizers you want to specialize in. Once you have made your choice, it's time to map out your favorite presets. These can be factory presets, third-party presets, or your own personal tweaked versions.

As I have mentioned earlier, most soft synths now come with a favoriting function within their browsers. Rate your presets. There is nothing more frustrating than to remember a certain sound in your head while not being able to recall it in the midst of battle. Again, we are no longer about searching. We are masters of recalling neatly ordered tools and sounds. That tool shed needs to be extra tidy, y'all.

Being sound librarians, we have our sample libraries neatly organized with aptly named folders on our active hard drive. Bedroom super producers go a step further by using Kontakt's library browser to put their libraries in order of preference. There is no more scrolling, then, for 80 percent of our main composing tasks.

Mix as You Go

As you have noticed in the previous mixing and mastering section, I am a strong advocate of the mix-as-you-go technique. Of course, it has taken me close to fifteen years to perfect this art form.

I now go a step further and mix mentally each individual track before I even touch the keyboard. When I compose, I always start with a simple piano patch. As soon as I have a strong harmonic and melodic foundation, I start creating a palette of sounds to meet the following criteria:

- Timbre
- Texture
- Dynamics
- Rhythm
- Melody
- Harmony
- Form

Always remember this: choosing the right sounds—beat making—is the cornerstone of mixing. With a perfect arrangement, mixing as a sound correction exercise becomes almost unnecessary.

Timbre

This is the tone of a musical pitch. Is it bright and edgy or muffled and bassy? Fender Rhodes are mellower than acoustic grand pianos. Fender Stratocaster guitars can sound clean and bright or dirty and twangy, depending on the pickup configuration and amp settings used. Strike a balance in timbre qualities.

Texture

According to Wikipedia, "texture is often described in regard to the density, or thickness, and range, or width, between lowest and highest pitches, in relative terms as well as more specifically distinguished according to the number of voices, or parts, and the relationship between these voices."

Here are the three main types of textures:

- Monophonic: a single melody played with no accompaniment (without harmony)
- Homophonic: a single melody played with accompaniment (with harmony)
- Polyphonic: multiple melodies played simultaneously

In music for media, I would suggest keeping song texture to a minimum. Because there is likely going to be voice-over, you don't want complex counterpoint melodies.

Dynamics

This is the level of volume (loud or soft) and changes in the volume of the music. Again, balance is key (I'm starting to sound like a broken record here). You cannot make everything as loud as possible in a given arrangement. Percussive dynamics should also match your harmonic and melodic content in such a way that it creates cohesive waves of intensity.

Rhythm

This is the recurrence or pattern in time (Wikipedia). Folks, I will repeat this as much as I need to: keep it simple, stupid. Unless you are a percussion expert, one shall not exaggerate the use of polyrhythms. Drums should follow the main accompaniment. Bass should somewhat follow the kick drum and vice versa. Build a strong backbone (bass and drums) and do not stray too far from it, rhythmically speaking.

Melody

Melody is any linear succession of musical tones. In music for media, melodies are usually minimalistic in nature as you don't want to overpower a potential voice-over. A great example is a very popular type of piano arrangement often used in TV ad music. You start with the chords and introduce notes of the main melody very gradually over time. This makes the musical idea very easy to understand and to anticipate and helps you build emotion and complexity over time.

Harmony

This is the chord progression of your song. Music for media is very much pop music in its essence. Work around three or four chords for your main A part. B parts (chord changes) are fine, but experience has shown me that most customers like their songs simple and straight to the point. One should be able to grasp the harmonic base of the song within the first few seconds (and ideally find it catchy right away).

Form

This is the character of the arrangement based on the previous six elements. What story is your song telling? What feelings emanate from it? Is it a dark, drama-laden piece? Or maybe a light, upbeat, and joyful jingle? As soon as the melodic and harmonic foundation has been set, you should choose textures, rhythms, and tone to support the form of your composition. Use mixing as a creative tool to craft the right form.

Actual Mixing

Because I carefully choose each element of my compositions according to the seven concepts mentioned above, I have little or no mixing to do at the end of the creation process. I am obsessed with sonic quality and form factor.

When I compose, I constantly make subtle EQ and compression changes and add any effect that will carry my vision through. This helps me get excited about the product I'm developing. If you are a beginner, tackle only the seven pillars of music composition first. Then slowly incorporate EQing into your routine. The technical portion of music creation should *never* take anything away from proper songwriting habits. After a while, though, this technique will improve your speed of execution tenfold.

Song Classification System

Because you are going to start one or two new songs every day, you will need a way to manage ongoing composition files. Some songs may be finished, while some are just going to be rough sketches. You need a way to visualize form and level of completion without having to open the actual sessions.

Song-Naming Convention

I have seen the work of many producers, and here are the five main naming conventions I have noticed:

- Poetic name: a simple word or phrase describing the form/vibe of the composition
- Random name: a funny yet not very descriptive name in regards to the form
- Genre and number: Hip-Hop 002
- Date of composition: 04/12/16
- Numerical increments

When I start a new composition, I use a working title based on technical terms: "Ambient Guitar Tropical House." Once the song nears completion, I name it with a catchy, two- or three-word sentence that describes the form of the song and creates a sensory story around it.

Make the name as evocative as possible. For a tropical house song, I might go for something along the lines of "Surf's Up!" The sentence conveys ideas of adventure, travel, and exotic destinations and has an action ring to it.

My publisher can then attract potential customers using the verbal imagery to help customers know what to expect from the music. As we will see later on, song-naming is a very strategic marketing tool.

Song Folder Nomenclature

As you may have guessed, we are now song librarians as well. I remember searching for a long time to no avail in front of a client to play a beat I thought was perfect for his project. It's unprofessional and embarrassing. We don't want that to happen to you.

Here is the basic content architecture I suggest in order to avoid the pitfall of lost musical gems:

- Sketches: create a folder for the quick and unfinished ideas. Upon further elaboration, the song files will make their way to one of the project folders. In the meantime, color code the session folders according to their level of completeness (traffic-lights method).
- Project Folders: create folders for each customer (custom composition duties) as well as each publisher (marketplaces you signed a contract with). For publishers, color code your sessions to have a quick feel of your progress.

Create an *online* folder for songs that have been approved in order to archive the work that is now up for sale. It's a great way to keep your eyes on the prize: your unfinished work.

Color coding the folders helps you identify the level of completion from a bird's-eye view. This will keep you organized and motivated.

Within each session folder, you need a simple versioning nomenclature. "Song Name + Number" is my convention. Please do not fall into the trap of "Song Name + Final + Number" as it will become very confusing which edit to export. The biggest number should highlight which is the final product. Period.

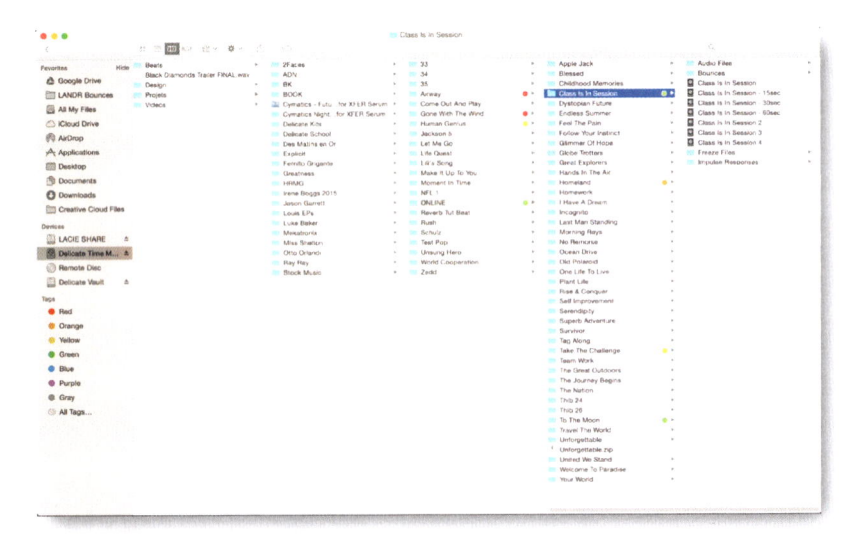

It's Like Managing an Airport

By now, you should be able to grasp just how much music you will be dealing with on a daily basis. As soon as songs hit that green light, they need to be submitted to your publishers. Managing these outgoing song files is like managing air or train traffic. Some shipments need to leave *now*, while some are not fully loaded yet. To help you keep your sanity and your computer desktop tidy, I have developed a visual way to classify outgoing song files. It looks like this:

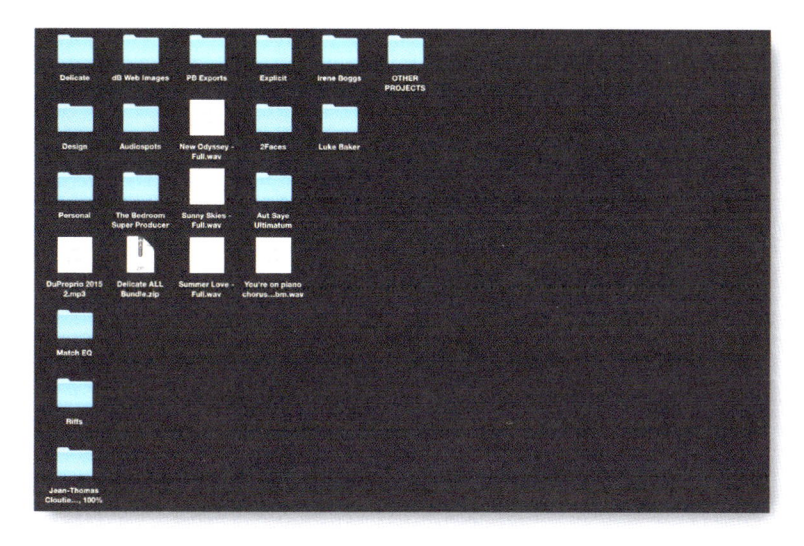

Each column refers to a project type:

- Personal marketing
- Customers
- Publishers
- Other projects

Starting from the top, the rank of a song signals its importance. The songs at the bottom have just been exported. They do not necessarily need to go right now. As they move to the top of the screen, the songs have either been sent or need to go fast. If they have been sent out, they should make their way to the project/publisher folder or to a sent folder. That way, our eyes are only concerned with the music that needs to depart.

Following the width/depth concept we have talked about earlier, I create columns based on the level of activity. Each of my publishers has its own column unless I'm only focusing on one publisher during a few months. The big clients (usually labels I have several ongoing projects with) get their own columns. I'll usually deal with the small clients (one to three songs) in one global column. I also have a column for my brand (marketing stuff mainly).

To-Dos

Management of to-do lists (yes, plural because you will have more than one list) is the final, overarching level of work management we need. These lists contain our ongoing projects, projects we have been procrastinating on, marketing tasks, and personal goals.

To stay on top of everything, I use a fantastic app called Clear. It's a no-nonsense app focused solely on creating lists—and guess what: it color codes the tasks based on the importance of the task (top tasks get closer and closer to red). The following image is my main music to-do list as it looks at the very moment I'm writing these words.

Keeping a list like this has two main advantages:

1. You will never drop the ball ever again.
2. You will get a sense of progress and motivation every day by deleting these tasks once completed.

As you can now tell, we want to empty our head as much as possible so that all the creative juices and brain power are used for one thing and one thing only: creating music.

CHAPTER 7
SOUND FUNDAMENTALS
WRITING MUSIC THAT MOVES PEOPLE

One does not simply write hundreds of catchy jingles every year without a method. That's why I make a point of helping you develop a sound work ethic.

Let's recapitulate:

- You understand that speed and efficiency are crucial in this business.
- You understand that by cutting repetitive tasks, you achieve speed and efficiency.
- You know that speed entails productivity. You will have to manage a lot of files. Therefore, you need a framework for classifying, naming, and sharing your work.
- You now have a framework as well as a wide array of tools to manage this newfound productivity.

At this stage, we have developed a set of sound fundamentals (pun intended). It's time to play ball.

But before we do, I would like to quickly debate simplicity versus complexity in music and discuss the concept of artistic ego. The following information on chords, scales, and melodies may sound complex for beginners and will surely be perceived as very elementary by seasoned musicians. My goal is for everyone to meet in the middle. Beginners *will* have to step their game up, and vets *will* have to dumb it down.

Beginners

You guys will benefit most from this information. It's time to go from instinct to actual knowledge of what you are doing musically and why. In your case, your ego will tell you that things have always worked out fine, so why learn basic music theory? Learn a little. It will go a long way.

Intermediate

You are in the same boat as I am. You know basic scales, chords, and intervals. Your ego will tell you that you know enough. But you do need to improve the richness and textures of your compositions. Keep learning new chords and figures every day.

Experts

Your group will have the biggest fight with the artistic ego. How many session players have I worked with, virtuosos even, who could not understand the process of dumbing down one's own musical ideas to fit in that box? Stock music buyers do not comprehend the depth of your musical knowledge. They buy music based on primal emotion. Why serve them caviar when all they really wanted was a good ol' cheeseburger?

So, again, let's all meet in the middle. Learn or unlearn, depending on your skill level. *Do not* underestimate this crucial step in your development as this may make you or break you.

Chord Progressions

Because emotion is so important to trigger sales in the marketplace, we want to pack your compositions with the strongest, boldest emotional messages possible. Within the first few seconds, the listener needs to be taken on a journey. And that, my friends, is done first by choosing a simple yet effective set of chords.

Allow me to repeat myself: music for media is pop music. It might be disguised as pop rock, classical, EDM, or hip-hop, but music for media is still written according to the universal laws of pop. There is an old adage in songwriting circles stating that 90 percent of pop songs follow the same chord progression structure. Let's analyze it.

I V VI IV

If you're not too familiar with musical scales and intervals, this might just look like hieroglyphs. They're actually Roman numerals for intervals between each of the four chords. One shall then read 1-5-6-4.

Let's take a basic musical scale: C major. "1-5-6-4" intervals from C then become C-G-Am-F. Play it on a keyboard, strum it on your guitar, or mouse it up in the piano roll. When you hear this chord progression, hundreds of songs will come to mind. That's exactly how we want our listeners to feel.

What's even better for us is that by only mangling the order of these four chords, we get altogether different feelings and vibes.

- I-V-VI-IV (C-G-Am-F): positive, upbeat, progress
- VI-IV-I-V (Am-F-C-G): sensitive, heroic, uplifting
- IV-I-V-VI (F-C-G-Am): sensitive, progress, nostalgia

There is room for debate as far as the emotions you will feel, but I think you get the idea. Countless pop hits have been made using just this one chord progression. Master it. Only then should you venture on to riskier terrain.

Scales and Modes

Now that we have a proven set of chords to play around, let's talk about the power of scales and modes. Yes, you could have a successful career by always using the C and Cm scales, but let's make it even more interesting.

Open your DAW. Input our infamous chord progression. Now make eleven copies of this four-chord loop. Move each copy up by one semitone. Do you notice the subtle changes in overall vibe and emotions? Transposing the loop (changing the mode) will do that.

I won't overwhelm you with musical theory. Just remember that you can tell a totally different (musical) story by just changing the scale. And because these scales and modes give us a brand-new set of "characteristic melodic behaviors" (Wikipedia), we are now ready to talk about our next fundamental skill: melody.

Melodies

Harmonic content gives us an idea of the feeling of a song as well as a basic blueprint for the rhythm section. Melodies tell the rest of the story. From now on, I want you to know which scale you wrote your basic chord progression in. That way, you know exactly which notes you are allowed to hit when writing your top melody.

I am often asked by beginner beat makers how to come up with great melodies. Here are my top five tips:

1. Listen to a lot of music in different genres, past and present.
2. Identify your scale.
3. Identify your rhythm.
4. Understand contour: ascending melodies for uplifting songs, descending for more emotional ones.
5. Understand intervals: when applying notes on top of your chords, start with basic intervals such as thirds and fifths, but experiment with other notes in the scale. Do this process by ear. Does it sound good? Does it clash?

In music for media, I have come to realize that you can tackle melodies in two ways: the anthem way or the minimalistic way.

Anthem

These types of tracks tell the whole story. They consist of very strong, upfront melodies. It is unlikely that you will get customers who need to put voice-over on the track. If the melody is strong enough, you will get sales. In my humble opinion, such a song will appeal to a smaller audience.

Minimalistic

We want you to make as many sales as possible on a consistent basis. Because there is a bigger market for voice-over-ready songs, you need to become an expert at these types of melodies. But what are they?

See them as tonal and harmonic embellishments on top of your chords. If your progression has four chords, it can take as little as four notes to make your progression sound unique and fresh. Try less. Try two notes. Minimalism in music for media goes a very long way.

On nights when you allow yourself to watch a little *Walking Dead* or *Game of Thrones*, pay close attention to the music used in commercials. Notice how simple yet effective the songs are. Notice how intensity is conveyed over time with just subtle melodic additions to the main ostinato or chord progression.

Rhythm and Groove

While there is nothing wrong with keeping each of your chords on the downbeats, part of making these well-known chord progressions unique and original is done with rhythm: when and where you play those chords. Experiment by playing chords longer or shorter and by pushing (rock) or dragging (funk) over the main rhythm.

If you're not a guitar or piano player, technology may actually give you an unfair advantage. There are now tons of apps and software writing all the MIDI for you, given that you know the chords to your song.

Chordbot

This nifty Android and iOS app (www.chordbot.com/) helps you build complete chord-based arrangements directly from your phone or tablet. The Pro version packs incredible features to enrich your songwriting experience. Best of all, you need little or no musical knowledge (well, maybe a good ear for what works).

Chordbot features include

- chord ordering (create your own progressions);
- chord selection and inversions (give new texture and tone to old chords);
- song section editor (carve out complete song structures);

- instrument selector (start playing around with tone, texture, and form);
- rhythm selector (automatically give different grooves to your progressions in real time); and
- export (yes, that's right—send the MIDIs to your workstation to carve out the details).

This app is a must-have. Because we are now more interested in the actual songwriting process and less concerned with computer-based production bells and whistles, this app could very well become the cornerstone of your whole composition framework. Write a few chords before bedtime. Wake up to a winning progression and simply flesh out the idea. No more blank staff syndrome.

EZKeys

If you like Chordbot, you are going to go crazy over this one too. The EZKeys line (https://www.toontrack.com/ezkeys-line/) consists of complete VST instruments ready to be loaded in your DAW for progression-based keyboard composition.

Very much like Chordbot, the software allows you to arrange chord progressions, choose variations and inversions, and have them played from a wide array of professional-sounding keyboard instruments (acoustic grands, electric pianos, organs, and so on).

Think Chordbot on steroids. The EZKeys instruments come packed with thousands of professionally played MIDI grooves to make your chords come alive. You will instantly feel like Bradley Cooper in *Limitless*. And once you are addicted, Toontrack has even more EZKeys instruments (new tones) and MIDI libraries (new textures) to keep you working for the next forty years. Need more reasons to take your chord game to the next level?

Now I know purists will want to burn me at the stake for even suggesting such heretic approaches to music composition. But let me put it this way:

- Survival is only certain through adaptation.
- Technology evolves very rapidly.
- Technology is nothing but a tool.
- Put your pride and ego aside.
- Try new tools every day.
- Don't die from future shock (shout out to Alvin Toffler).

Tones, Textures, and Form

Once you have found a set of chords and a single melody (you only need one) that sound great with a simple piano sound, it is time to dress it up.

Remember how I talked about telling a story through sound? Your goal is to paint a picture so rich and beautiful that content creators will see right away which images would match your musical portrait.

Layering

Layering is the process of having multiple instruments, or layers of sound, playing the same part to achieve original and rich-sounding tones. Texture is technically achieved by more complex chords and counter melodies, but because music for media needs to stay as simple and straight to the point as possible (at least in my experience), layering can trick the mind of the listener by making simple musical ideas sound big and epic.

Try this at home:

1. Create a set of three or four staccato chords.
2. Duplicate your MIDI loop, load a spiccato string ensemble patch, and move the chords up one octave while keeping the bass notes in the lower octaves. Double the bass notes so that they are played by both the double basses and the cellos.
3. Sounds good? Let's keep layering sounds.
4. Duplicate the MIDI track again and load a staccatissimo brass ensemble patch. Delete notes in your chords so that the brass only plays fifths.
5. Double the bass melody played by the piano and strings with a timpani patch.

You just went from a simple piano chord progression to an epic Hollywood sound in a matter of minutes, all thanks to a little MIDI wizardry.

Try the same thing on melodies. The goal is to find tones that complement each other both in tone and register (octaves).

Lessons learned

I'm trying to build the strongest case for a pop music approach to give you the best chances of succeeding in this market.

If you're a jazz pianist, revisit the I-IV-V-VI progression and add your own twist. Train your brain to find beauty in simplistic ideas (and yes, my use of the term "simplistic" is somewhat pejorative).

If you learned everything on your own and have a great ear, speed up your learning process with one of the tools I mentioned earlier. The goal is for everyone to know where they reside on the musical ability spectrum, so it becomes easy to focus on the proper learning tasks.

Again, let's all meet in the middle.

But because I like to keep things interesting, we are now going to learn how stock music is also not pop music. Let me show you what I mean.

CHAPTER 8

POP BUT NOT POP

FORMATTING YOUR MUSIC FOR MEDIA

Let's see where we are at:

- You have developed techniques that speed up your creative process tenfold.
- You now write music based on tried and tested musical formulas.
- Creativity finds you on a weekly basis.

Now let's make these musical gems work for your targeted audience.

The Edits Game

Let's make a little paradigm shift.

Typical Pop Song Format
intro/verse/chorus/verse/chorus/bridge/chorus/outro
or:
intro/verse/hook/chorus/verse/hook/chorus/bridge/chorus/outro

Contrary to pop music, transitions between song sections happen more gradually and organically in music for media. Buildups are longer. Let us picture in our minds an intensity curve that rises and falls very smoothly to allow video creators to benefit from changes in mood and intensity without having to drastically alter the flow and rhythm of images.

Song Editing Tips

- *Song edits are weapons you can use to highlight very specific details of your compositions.*
- *Each edit should sound like a full song, meaning it has an intro, a build-up, a climax, a breakdown, and an outro. Rise, sustain, and then fall.*

As I've mentioned earlier, music for media should be seen as pop music in the sense that it is simple and catchy.

Because our audience consists of media makers and not artists, we will have to think differently when formatting, sequencing, and arranging our songs. Content creators will need specific song formats that are standards in advertising, television, and radio.

Publishers will usually ask for the following edits (or cues) when accepting a song in their catalogs:

- Full song
- Sixty seconds
- Thirty seconds
- Fifteen seconds
- Five-second stinger
- Loops

Full Song

The full song is the most important edit in your arsenal. This cue is going to be showcased first on your publisher's website, and buyers will decide upon this one as to whether or not to buy your song. Make it count.

This is what the full song edit looks like for my best-selling track "Greatness":

To listen to the song and edits, go to premiumbeat.com and type in "Delicate Beats Greatness" in the search box on the homepage.

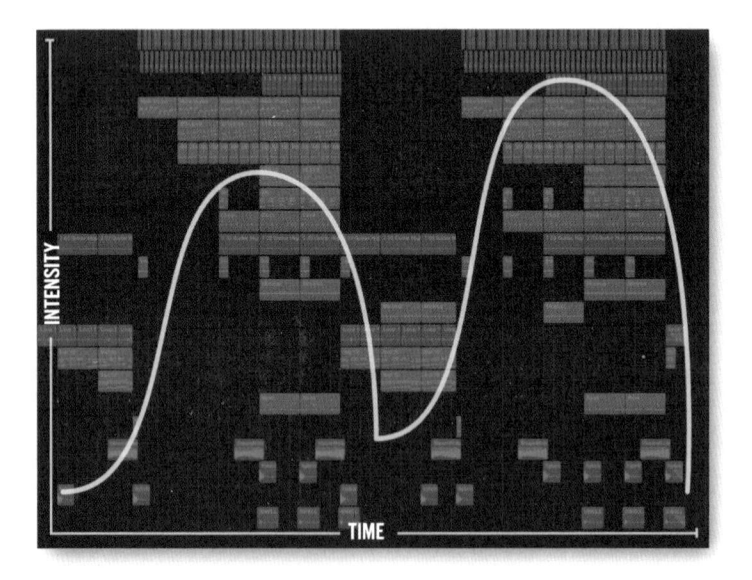

Notice the following:

- The first buildup starts lower than the second in terms of intensity.
- Buildups lead very gradually to each climax by adding subtle elements every four bars.
- The second climax is more intense than the first one.
- There is no outro, just a big boom.

The full song edit should last anywhere between two and three minutes. As a rule of thumb, try to create two sequences of build/climax/breakdown.

Another very effective technique consists of creating the exact opposite intensity curve: superfast buildups leading to climaxes and very slow and gradual fadeouts into what we call breakdowns (low-intensity musical beds usually with less percussions and drums).

Sixty Seconds
This edit builds only once and can usually just be the first half of your full song. Start high and slowly fade out or start low, rise gradually, and finish on an emphatic boom.

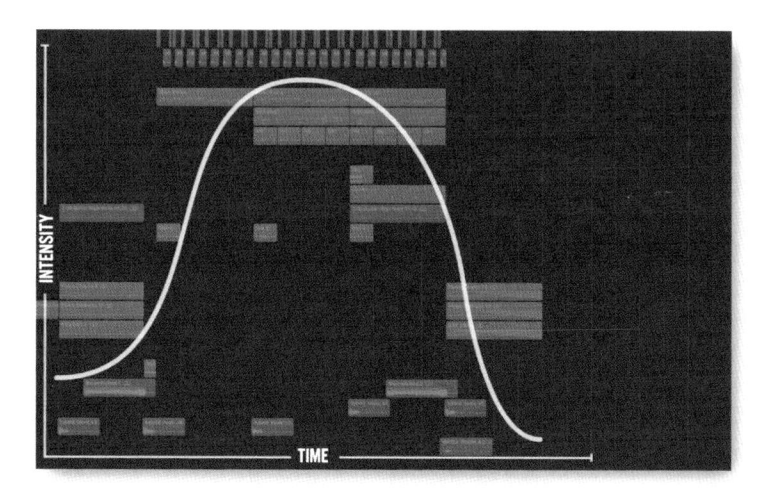

Notice the following:

- I'm using only the last four bars of my full song intro.
- I'm using all twelve bars of my climax sections.
- The outro consists of the first four bars of the intro.

- Sixty percent of the cue is action packed with quick buildups and breakdowns.
- This edit makes room for vocals at the beginning and very end only.

To help you carve out meaningful edits, think in terms of voice-over:

- Is the fictitious ad starting with an energetic mix of video and music to make way for the voice-over after the first climax? If so, this climax should not be too long. Something like eight bars would work well and transition in the marketing speech fast enough.
- Does the ad start with a gentle music bed with voice-over? If so, build your bed over thirty-two bars and finish the cue with an emotionally packed arrangement.
- Always make sure smooth transitional elements such as reversed cymbals and Fx swooshes lead in and out of your cue.

Thirty Seconds

This edit has the same format as the sixty-second edit. You can choose to have either a longer climax for more action-packed cues or a longer buildup/breakdown for mellow, emotional cues.

In the following example, thirty seconds was not enough to highlight the two main sections of my climax, so I chose to highlight the first section, which is more minimalistic in terms of layers of sound. It made more sense musically to go from the simple intro to this section. Sometimes great impact comes from sparseness.

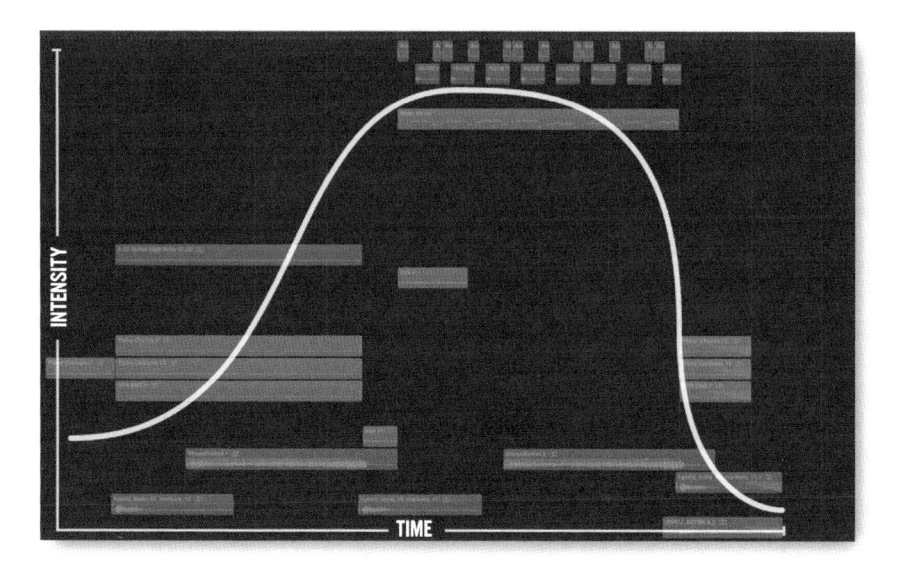

Notice the following:

- I'm keeping the same intro as in the sixty-second cue.
- I use only the first section of the climax.
- I created a custom two-bar outro playing the first chord of my progression but with a newly added chord that resolves within those two bars.
- Half of the cue is setting the mood, while the other half sets the tone for action shots.

Fifteen Seconds

I know, I know: you can't tell the full story in just fifteen seconds. This is why the fifteen-second cue is so strategic.

You must make an important choice between your intro and climax elements. This cue is either all action or all mood. Make the call based on your full song cue.

In the case of "Greatness," I chose the first four bars of my climax section, ending on the same emphatic boom. That way, my strongest section is showcased on all edits.

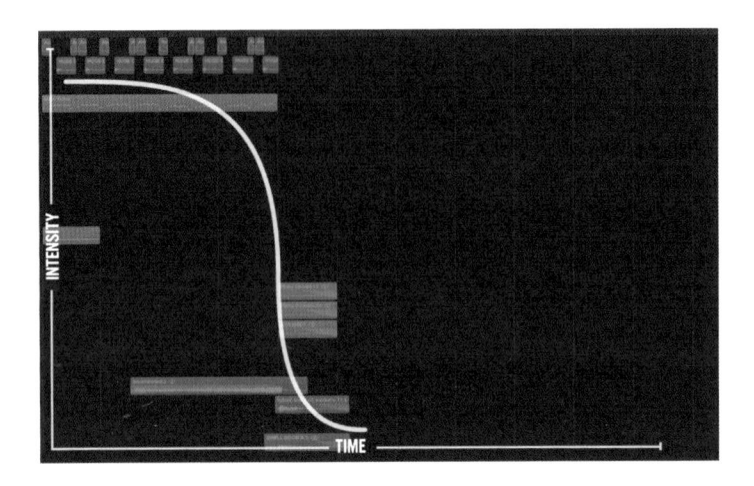

Notice the following:

- There is no buildup before the climax section.
- The song does not finish only on a percussive boomer. Instead, it quickly breaks down using the two-bar custom outro of the thirty-second cue.

Song Edits Tip
Create your edits starting with the longest while keeping all elements of the composition in the session. Simply move those on the right of the arrange window, roughly sixteen bars further. That way, you have all the building blocks at your fingertips to try out several combinations before deciding which version of the edit has the greatest impact.

Stinger
This edit lasts approximately five seconds and usually will consist of the ending portion of your fifteen-second cue. Use a fast, sweeping

effect as an intro and rapidly hit the listener with your first or final chord layered with percussion and sound effects.

Loops

Break down your full song edit into four- to eight-bar loops. Loops work better in video editing software if they are exported without the transitional sound effects (cymbal swells, drum fills, and the like).

Try as much as possible to create loops that do not evolve over time in order for the cue to loop seamlessly.

This is how I chopped up my "Greatness" full song cue:

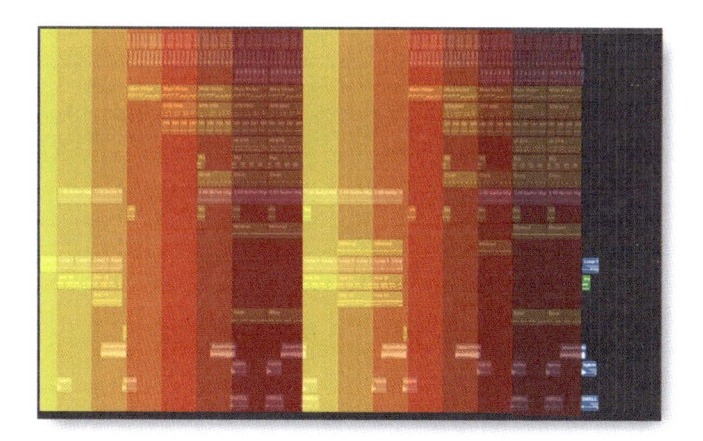

Loops Tips

Mute your sound effects and transition percussions. If you automate filters, try as much as possible to incorporate the full automation into one loop. Do not make loops much longer than sixteen bars of music.

Lessons learned

The art of the cue is subtle and its power should not be underestimated. It's a great sales multiplier.

Aside from the tips I have given you, I invite you to listen to your competition as well as TV ads and YouTube videos. Listening to music and watching video at the same time paints the true picture of how music should be sequenced for content creators.

We are trying to make these people's jobs easier every step of the way, as you will discover in the next chapter.

CHAPTER 9

INSPIRE THE CREATIVES

BECOMING YOUR OWN PERSONAL MARKETING GURU

Where are we at?

- Your music paints pictures and stories to inspire content creators.
- Your edits pack a punch and highlight the strengths of your music.
- Your cues make a video editor's job a dream come true.
- Your product is ready for the big show.

Inspiring the creatives is done in two ways:

1. By creating instantly enjoyable, simple yet effective pieces of music;
2. By putting words in the content creators' heads to complete your artistic vision and convince them of buying your wonderful music.

To complete step two, you will

- become your own marketer;
- understand the power of keywords and metadata; and
- write song titles and marketing copy that will compel buyers to listen to your work and understand your artistic vision.

Song Titles

I love to start my days listening to motivational YouTube clips using excerpts from Eric Thomas or Les Brown talks. Video creators usually combine these talks with tracks from Audiomachine or 2 Steps From Hell, two of the biggest players in the Hollywood trailer game. Man, I love their work.

When I started my "Greatness" session, I knew I had to try my hand at one of these epic motivational tracks.

To create a niche for my product, I decided to drastically slow down the tempo (from 135 to 85 bpm) and instead of creating a typical trailer song, I composed a hip-hop anthem with Queen-esque, bone-crushing drums. I was lucky enough to be the first composer to submit this kind of track to my publisher, and this, in turn, created a very special appeal to its customers. Needless to say, "Greatness" still pays the rent. Handsomely too, I might add.

My working title was "Go Big or Go Home." It was a pretty good title. When I uploaded the track to my publisher's servers, the engine alerted me that the title was already taken. It wasn't a huge surprise as these common sayings/catchphrases are *great* for song titles.

I needed something that would be simple enough to convey hope, motivation, and strength. I also wanted an overarching term that would illustrate the ultimate goal that athletes strive for: greatness.

This is no fluke. I had done my research and realized that 90 percent of these motivational videos used one-word, uplifting, and inspirational terms such as this one. I also knew this would work as these videos all have millions of views.

Here are a few things to look out for when choosing titles:

- Choose very short sentences (one to four words).
- Use sayings and well-known catchphrases whenever possible.
- They should be emotionally charged (funny, mysterious, or inspiring).
- It should be highly descriptive of the song's mood and form.
- It should be simple to spell, therefore more likely to be used in the search engine.

Song Descriptions

Some publishers will write their own song descriptions, but in most cases, this is your job. Marketing copy 101 alert: make sure you fill this space with emotionally charged keywords—yes, keywords. You want your customers to find your song first, so get inside their heads and find the terms they will most likely use to find your song using the website's search engine.

Here is the "Greatness" description (as written by the premiumbeat.com crew): "Light with pulsing piano that builds to a heavy hip-hop groove, dramatic strings and punchy percussion that creates a bold and confident mood." In roughly twenty words, they aptly describe the whole arrangement of the full song edit while packing it with strong keywords such as "hip-hop," "bold," and "confident."

Premiumbeat.com has an editorial guideline to make all descriptions neutral in tone. When I write song descriptions for other websites, I fill the writing with my personal tone. I write it as if it were a twenty-word slogan. It has to pack in everything from humor and drama to intrigue or action. Make it witty. Make it count.

Metadata

Metadata are keywords allowing the website to store more information regarding the musical piece's tone, form, instruments, and moods. These keywords are used for website navigation and search purposes.

Once again, let's take a look at "Greatness" and analyze its metadata:

Genre(s)
Action, adventure, hip-hop, production/film scores, trailer, urban

Mood(s)
Action, sports, adventure, discovery, suspense, drama

Instrument(s)
Drums, handclaps, piano, strings

Tag(s)
Action, bold, dramatic, powerful, determined, trailer, cinematic, tension, building, confident, urgent

Easier Said Than Done

Most websites have fully loaded keyword libraries that you can readily choose from. Make sure you use the best of the best. As you know by now, it's not just about making evocative music. You have to sell it. Titles, descriptions, and metadata are your trusted allies for the job.

With certain publishers asking for a *lot* of metadata, uploading songs can become very time consuming. I strongly advise you to create song upload templates (I know my methods are somewhat template happy). Some sites even offer this functionality. If not, keep a spreadsheet of keywords you can quickly copy and paste, based on the type of cue you are uploading.

To simplify your copywriting duties, focus your compositional work around four or five cue genres—for example, hip-hop, corporate electronic, pop folk jingles, movie trailer, and so on.

There is always dirty work. In our specific case, this is it. Don't worry; you will become a well-oiled machine, and, in no time, marketing your songs on marketplaces will become second nature.

Metadata Tip

Do not take metadata lightly. Some publishers have hundreds of thousands of music cues on their servers. If you want your diamond in the rough to be found, you'd better make sure it's easier to find through search and navigation. Use a thesaurus or a synonym/antonym dictionary; look at the best sellers' descriptions and metadata. Find any and all keywords that might help your song come to the surface.

Pricing

I work with several publishers. Some have fixed pricing, while some let composers set their prices manually. Pricing, just like copywriting and metadata capturing, is an art form. It is not as simple as selling an item a few dollars below your competition. As a matter of fact, this practice will most likely undervalue your product and hurt your business.

I am no expert in this field, but here are a few tips:

- Measure your product's quality with your competition's and price accordingly.
- Strike a balance: do not over- or underprice.
- Profit margin: if a beat took you a month to finalize, price it higher. Older beats that sat around for a while can be under-priced (a little).
- Create cohesive pricing ratios between your edits, for example:
  o Full song: forty dollars
  o Loops set: thirty dollars
  o Sixty seconds: twenty dollars
  o Thirty seconds: ten dollars
  o Fifteen seconds: five dollars
- Keep it tidy. Your pricing should not look random across your whole catalog. Prepare two pricing tables: standard pricing and a cheaper one for rebates.

Lessons learned

Choosing titles. Writing song descriptions. Defining song attributes and metadata.

This is by far the most tedious task in a media composer's day.

At the same time, it is our greatest weapon to convey our full artistic vision. We all see things when we compose. Colors. Movies. People.

This marketing copy is our way of letting videographers know what went on inside our heads when we composed our little gems. This is our way of connecting to our buyers in order to combine creative forces and create timeless pieces of art. It's the final step we have a little control over before throwing our bottle in the ocean.

On a less poetic note, keywords and descriptions are what gets our music sold. Period.

CHAPTER 10

BEYOND STOCK MUSIC
MULTIPLE STREAMS OF MUSICAL INCOME

Yes, what I promise in this book is too good to be true. It really is. I am humbled every day to be able to live my dream making music *and* get paid handsomely doing it.

With that being said, the stock music game was never my only stream of income. It should not be yours either. Let's talk business diversification.

A Strong Presence and Brand

If you put great music out for sale in marketplaces, people will seek you out for custom composing jobs and other business opportunities. They need to be able to find you easily. For that to happen, you need a strong web presence.

More importantly, they need to trust you. And for that to happen, you need a strong brand.

Branding is outside the scope of this book, but I want to quickly touch upon a few important points. Quite frankly, online music production is plagued with poor choices in this department, so I want to help my colleagues out.

While this exercise does not have a direct impact on the quality of your music, it will have strong repercussions on your ability to create new income sources outside of stock music.

A Timeless Logo

Before making the shift to music full time, I was an artistic director and web ergonomics expert, so I know a thing or two about branding and logo design. To start the branding process, find a catchy production moniker and match it with a timeless logo. What makes a timeless logo? I'm glad you asked.

Simplicity

Some people think a logo is wallpaper. It is not. Make sure it looks great in black and white. That's black shapes over a white background, with no shades of gray. Shrink it. Are the type and symbol legible when tiny?

Memorability

Beware of the clichés such as piano keys, MPC pads, G-clef symbols, and the like. Make yourself stand out. Tell a different story with your logo. Create a brand that is a direct extension of your music-making process.

Endurance

If you checked the two previous boxes, your logo should withstand the test of time. The Delicate Beats logo is now twenty years old. It has always been a feather with a simple typeface and has been redesigned only once (I created a slicker, more geometric version of the feather and changed the font accordingly two years ago).

Versatility

To this day, the Delicate Beats logo is my best logo work. Why? Not because it's the cutest or flashiest. It works everywhere, every time. Understand that your logo will be seen on computer screens, phones, tablets, business cards, letter heads, T-shirts, hats, and so on. Use simple shapes and simple typefaces.

Appropriateness

Like me, you might have started out as a hip-hop/urban producer. While guns and violent imagery may appeal to rappers, our new clientele might feel different about it. You are now going to go back and forth with VPs and CEOs. Name and design accordingly.

Hold your logo and brand to the highest standards. Nobody cares anymore if you are a one-person army operating from a tiny corner in your bedroom. The only things that matter are the results, and you have them to prove your worth.

If you are not a graphic designer, pay the good folks at 99designs.com or even Fiverr.com a visit, and get help from a professional. Your career depends on it.

A Strong Brand

The logo is your company's signature. The brand is its public image and personality. While the logo may be the cornerstone, the brand is the big picture that encompasses it all. Give attention to all details.

Define Your Personality

Are you young and hip? Mature and calm? Dark and mysterious? This step is crucial because it will dictate all actions you are going to take in building a cohesive, strong brand.

Define Your Vision

Do you want to be perceived as a personalized boutique music studio or a big, corporate powerhouse? Where do you see yourself in five years? Are you going to expand into drum kits and Internet mixing services? Build a road map.

Communicate with Personality and Confidence

You know these Twitter spammers who advertise five beats for a few dollars many times a day? How do you perceive these offers?

While there is nothing wrong with giving big discounts to returning customers, giving away your hard work undervalues your brand a great deal. That's wrong. You want the public's perception to hold your brand in the highest regard.

Be assertive. Be funny. Be smart. Be useful. Post quality content. The Internet is a public place. Do you want to be seen begging, or do you want customers to beg for your premium knowledge, products, and services?

Your Own.com

A strong Internet brand needs a strong web presence. The first strategic step in building this presence is achieved by creating your own website. No, it's not free, and, yes, it's very important. Potential clients who hear my music on my publishers' websites almost never contact me through social media; they fill out the contact form at delicatebeats.com.

The musical alias you use on the marketplace needs to match your domain name or vice versa. Make it simple and stupid for people to find you without having them worry if you are the same person who composed such and such songs.

A professional website is a perfect vehicle for you to showcase your past work, but it is especially useful to develop the other streams of income for your music business.

If you are interested in selling products, Shopify is an incredible content and e-commerce management system. Buy yourself a great-looking premium template and look sharp every time a new customer knocks at your door.

Not ready for e-commerce? Not comfortable with web design or front-end programming? No problem. Get going now with Squarespace.com. The templates are simply gorgeous, and the page editing tools are made for people with no knowledge or skills. I know WordPress is much more flexible, but do you really want to enter into screaming matches with your computer to embed a video in a product description? Music and brand first. You will always have time later to make your web infrastructure more sophisticated.

The Money Is in the List

In Internet marketing circles, there is a popular saying about the list: "The money is in the list." What list am I talking about?

This is the list of your current and potential customers' e-mail addresses. That's right—nothing is more important in Internet sales and marketing than the power to speak directly to your clients. It is way more powerful than likes and social media followers—trust me.

Build your list now. We all start too late, and it's a damn shame. To build your list, you will need a website on which you can create an opt-in form. This form will be linked to your e-mail marketing platform. Create a Mailchimp or Aweber account now. Not tomorrow… now!

The Social Network

Last but not least, round up your Internet presence by taking part in the conversation. Be present on the main social networks.

In order of importance, we have the following:

1. YouTube: This is the number-two most-visited website after Google. If you have something to promote, showcase, or sell, start there. Give away free beats. Post free tutorials. Give talks about music-related topics.
2. Instagram: Marketing consultants are now urging their clients to market themselves and their products on Instagram. I urge you too. Show your music creation process. Post photos of your gear. Inspirational quotes are huge these days. Video is also slated to become the most important type of content on the gram.
3. Facebook: While this is the third most-visited website on earth, it is more difficult to get your point across because of all the noise. Nonetheless, you need to tell your story there too. Duplicate your YouTube videos and promote them. Create links to your website to send traffic (blog posts, product pages, and so forth).
4. Twitter: If you have time and energy left after taking your marketing seriously on the first three platforms, Twitter is still a great way to post quality content and quotes and to publish your offers.

Social media is a lot of work. That's why I leave out platforms such as Periscope and Snapchat for now.

Thankfully, you can create publishing links between all of them. Here is a great chain I use for my YouTube videos:

1. Post a video to YouTube.
2. Create a blog post on your site, embedding the video as well as writing a thorough description of the video's topic (keywords, baby).
3. Create video snippets for Instagram and give the link in your bio. Make sure your Instagram posts are posted automatically to Facebook and Twitter.
4. Create screenshots of the video with the title in it for Instagram.
5. Send traffic from your Facebook producer page to the blog post.
6. Send traffic from your Twitter account to the blog post.
7. After a week or two, duplicate the video on your Facebook page. Facebook wants your videos to be native, so it's better than embedding them. Sponsor these posts if you have loose change.

Vision. Brand. Website. Email list. Social-media presence. Personality, quality, and involvement. Work on these major keys daily, and I promise that you will create a sturdy foundation for your Internet-based cash cow.

There are no shortcuts. Trust me, I have searched for them, tried them, and failed miserably. A little quality content every day goes a very long way. You now know what kind of voodoo is required to make you famous online. Nothing fancy, just true genuineness and passion.

Let's now explore ways to create new streams of income.

Milking the Creative Cow

I apologize for this long branding interlude, but I had to get on my Mr. Miyagi shit for a minute. Unless you develop great branding skills now, you are going to have a very tough time developing other areas of your online music business.

Let's pretend you are now successful in the stock music game (it pays some bills), and you have a good Internet presence and brand. What's next?

Luckily for you, there are already tons of items sitting on your hard drive that you can now sell, thanks to the countless hours you have spent crafting music and sounds.

Drum Kits

By now, you must have noticed the explosion of this industry. And explosion is not an understatement: people are making six-figure incomes selling drum kits online. Even the biggest names in the game feel compelled to jump on the bandwagon.

Because you are a producer who takes his or her craft to heart, I know you have developed a distinct and powerful drum sound. These sounds are neatly ordered and classified because you, my friend, are a professional sound librarian. It's time to gather those sounds and create an attractive package:

- Name all files aptly.
- Brand these babies with a mouthwatering name and design.
- Create a comprehensive YouTube demo.
- Find marketplaces.
- Sell, sell, sell.

My only recommendation is to keep your stuff original and unique. There is nothing more frustrating than buying a drum kit with sounds you have already purchased somewhere else.

Here are a few tips on how to create a unique drum kit:

- Focus on creating usable sounds out of the box.
- Layer, EQ, distort, and mangle your base sounds with your own unique drum mixing techniques.
- Record your own sounds and layer them with some or your go-to sounds to create rich textures.
- Use your newly acquired librarian skills to create a folder architecture that will help producers find the right sounds for the job.
- Paint a story for the buyers: choose a name and visual that complement the types of sounds you have created (beware of making it sound gimmicky).

Synth Presets

If you are using industry-leading software synthesizers such as Massive, Sylenth, or Serum and have a knack for creating your own custom sounds, there is a market for those as well. The more popular the software synthesizer, the bigger the potential customer base.

Here are some steps to start selling your preset packs:

- Name your presets by sound type: bass, leads, chords, pads, Fx, and so forth.
- Create killer artwork and themes.
- Create relationships with marketplaces geared toward your genre of music.

- Stay ahead of the curve by designing sounds for new emerging styles.
- Focus on patch usability and musicality.

Kontakt Libraries

I am an avid Kontakt user. It makes up 90 percent of my VST usage. What I love about Kontakt libraries, aside from the fantastic realism, is the experience of working with a themed user interface dedicated to making the samples come to life.

Kontakt programmers now achieve things that were unthinkable only a few years ago. As producers start to see the infinite potential of software samplers coupled with the incredible power of modern computers, demand and offers alike are soaring. Don't get me wrong: the overhead on programming Kontakt libraries is very high at first, but the reward is equally high.

Here is what you will need in order to create successful Kontakt libraries:

- Develop unique library concepts from sample sources to scripting.
- Create beautiful, highly intuitive user interfaces that are direct extensions of your library brand. I highly recommend working with a user-experience expert.
- Use KSP scripting to make your library as musical and playable as possible. Find a programmer. I doubt that you will want to go down the same path I took and read the whole manual, scour every last forum post, and spend long, frustrating nights debugging your hundreds of lines of code.

Templates

Here is a simple example: "Tropical House track reminiscent of Kygo in Ableton Live 9, packed with exclusive Massive presets and Live macros. 108 bpm."

DAW-specific and genre-based templates are such incredible learning tools for less experienced producers. Without doing anything, you can teach thousands of people how to automate effects, mix genre-specific sounds, and arrange full, professional-sounding songs.

Templates are also a great way to cross-promote your other products. Throw in a few drum sounds from your latest drum kit, two or three synth presets, and you might just create new customers for these two related products.

To create templates, simply revive and clean up old tracks. Name all the tracks neatly, create a killer mix/master, and tweak your patches so the final product sounds current enough for young cats to take notice. To market it, record a short screencast where you play the track while highlighting tricks the buyers will learn when opening the session file.

Premium Video Courses

Here are a few ideas to create useful video courses that people will pay to see:

- Overall or genre-specific mixing masterclasses
- Overall or genre-specific mastering masterclasses
- Software synthesizer masterclasses
- DAW-specific editing techniques
- Genre-specific programming techniques

A great way to cross-promote products is by selling a video course companion to your song templates. That way, you can create a three-option product: the template, the video course, and the premium bundle including the course and the template as well as all the samples and synth presets. Talk about a killer offer!

Market your courses by giving away the first few minutes on YouTube. Free content is an amazing branding and marketing tool: you create value and a hook for potential buyers.

Once you have established yourself as an authority with a particular DAW and music genre(s), people will gravitate toward you. They will develop a thirst for your knowledge and sounds. Other service-based business opportunities will present themselves.

As I want this book to be only about automated income sources, I will not discuss audio services such as mixing, mastering, teaching, and consulting. All I'm going to mention is be prepared. Have offers and pricing for those as well. If you have the time, they are also great ways to monetize your talent(s). Last bit of advice: if connecting with people through your services is your thing, visit Airgigs.com. Yup, there are marketplaces for audio services too.

The Placement Game

I want to end this segment on monetizing your craft by offering my views on the holy grail of music production: getting placements with major artists.

We all have this dream of producing tracks for big names. When I talk to younger producers, I always point out the potential pitfall: the major placements game is like the lottery. Only a handful wins.

It's easy to spend countless hours creating tracks, shopping them around, and getting little to no substantial results (dollars). Do not think a manager will change anything. The only way you are ever going to get major placements is by producing major-placement-sounding music. Period. By then, you won't even need a manager because your music will be undeniable.

I have come to realize that A&Rs detect a hit only if it is one. They will seldom (if ever) see potential in an unfinished but promising idea. Earn your stripes. Put in the time and effort.

Here is what I suggest: create a steady source of automated online income first. Once you have money rolling in each week and start to pay your bills, create some free time each week to experiment and develop that next big sound. Pay the bills first and then chase your fame-and-fortune dreams.

CHAPTER 11
COMPOSER SELF-HELP
CREATING A LIFESTYLE THAT WILL HELP YOU THRIVE

Composing music every day is not easy. Composing high-quality, broadcast-sounding material every day is difficult. Withstanding this kind of effort over several years is a science.

I remember my first six months. I was so happy to finally be living my dream—*the* dream. My energy level was inhuman. I worked twelve-hour days, six days a week for six months straight. Guess what happened then?

I crashed. *Hard.*

Luckily for me, I had planned two business/leisure trips in the summer following these first six months, which allowed me to recuperate. I was still making music part time, but it helped me get perspective on my work routine and overall lifestyle. Shout out to the Hollywood Hills and Canadian Rockies!

When I got back home, I enrolled in Tai Lopez's 67 Steps program as well as his personal MBA course. Sometimes, with self-help, you read a book or enter a program hoping to unlock a particular secret of the universe only to finally get out and realize that the simple truth was staring at you all along.

That's when it hit me: my music game was on par. Everything else around it just did not support such a mentally demanding and creativity-draining job.

I then set out to establish a plan that would allow me to incrementally improve all areas of my life. Tai calls this the "sculptor's approach." Instead of overhauling your whole life in a very short time (which is not sustainable), the sculptor's approach consists of chipping away tiny pieces (bad habits) every day. This makes it very easy to incorporate lasting changes in your lifestyle, and it is much less stressful on the body, mind, and spirit.

The Seven Pillars

"Do you know what's the difference between me and you? You practice gymnastics. I practice everything."

— SOCRATES

This quote from the movie *Peaceful Warrior* changed my life. I went from practicing computer music to practicing everything else. A few years ago, I started to buy books, study, and experiment on the following seven areas of my lifestyle to improve my vitality, focus, and overall endurance. The body is a temple. Keep it clean.

Nutrition

One of the most fulfilling discussions I ever had with my dad was about life hygiene as a whole. My dad had cancer very early on in his life, and I guess it really showed him the value of taking care of oneself holistically. So when I ventured into the uncharted territory of musical Internet entrepreneurship, he made sure I understood the importance of cleansing the spirit, the mind, *and* the body to stay on top of my game.

The way I see it, nutrition is at the very center of this life hygiene idea. "You are what you eat," they say. Well, if that's the case, a bedroom super producer ought to optimize his or her diet to maximize focus time and quality.

I have been all over the place, from raw vegan, to vegetarian, to pescatarian, to full-on beef eater, and back. In the process, I found this one universal, major key to success: find your equilibrium. It's OK to hit McDeez once in a while on a cheat day. Just remember this: as long as you document your eating habits and try to improve them by a little every day, you're going to be just fine. I will end this section on a second incredible quote by my man, Hippocrates:

> *Let food be thy medicine and medicine be thy food.*

Exercise

The number-two pillar is to keep the body active. They say the secret to longevity is to break a sweat every day. It's easier said than done!

The benefits of an active lifestyle are pretty much endless:

- Vitality
- Physical shape (duh!)

- Mental health
- Better stress management
- Higher self-esteem

We have all been there. You get your gym membership, you go five times a week in the first month, and then you never go back. The next year, you try again and fail.

The reality is this: if you're a music producer, chances are the gym is too big a time commitment in your day. You would rather put on a few pounds than miss an extra one or two hours every day pounding on those pads. I don't blame you.

I live on the third floor of an apartment building, so noise is also an issue. One day, by pure accident, I stumbled upon the solution to all of these problems: fitness apps on my Apple TV and, more specifically, calisthenics.

Calisthenics, in essence, is body-weight training. That means you can crush pretty much any muscle in total silence. J. T.—1, gym—0.

Armed with this newfound knowledge, I started to browse Apple TV and online fitness apps to find the best app and calisthenics home workout. It turned out that I found a two-part calisthenics training with codyapp.com for just fifty-nine dollars. That means I get two lifetime subscriptions to full programs for the price of one month of gym membership. You heard me.

Better yet, these programs represent no more than twenty-five minutes of my time per day and target muscles you have probably never even heard of. I have been doing the Complex Foundations and Complex Builder, by Darrell Michnowicz, for the past year or so, and I can honestly say I have never gotten a more complete workout in my life: 2–zip.

Darrell just put out his newest and toughest program yet: the Pyramid. So guess what I'm getting myself for Christmas this year?

Take Out the Trash

The trash is the negative thoughts we entertain daily, stopping us from achieving greatness.

I once had a mentor who urged all of his students to get rid of their "loser mentality." As artists, we are all somehow deeply insecure. We want to be liked. We want our work to be recognized by fans and peers alike. Because of these fears, we fill our minds with poison for our creativity. Every day.

"You will never sound as good as such and such production superstars." "This guy is half your age and has already put out two albums." "Maybe Mom was right; I shouldn't have quit my day job."

Sound familiar? That's not you. That's your ego creating a mental loser persona to protect you from failing. This defense mechanism is perfectly normal. Hell, it is even healthy to a certain degree.

Once you sit down in front of the computer, guitar, or piano, though, this internal discourse has to vanish altogether to make way for divine inspiration. Here are a few techniques I use to rid my mind of the mental trash before, during, and after musical sessions.

Meditation

I have read countless books on Buddhism, transcendental meditation, and all things (mental) yoga. At the end of the day, you do not need to read books and go to seminars to understand and practice meditation. Simply close your eyes, breathe, and listen quietly to your ego talking. If you don't know how to do it, here's my trick: when the loser talks, do not answer. When you get better at it, start to deny the loser altogether. When he or she speaks, quiet him or her down. If the silent technique is too difficult at first, you can also listen to guided meditations on YouTube or apps such as Headspace.

Reading

After enrolling in Tai Lopez's 67 Steps program, I realized I was doing something right with my life: I read a lot. Better yet, I found room for improvement: reading with a purpose. Whatever goal you set for yourself, read a book on exactly that. Or two. Or three.

A great starting point is to read motivational material to shape your inner super producer. Start with classics such as *Think and Grow Rich*. You will achieve things you did not think were possible, but the first step is always to make mental room for these ideas to be cultivated daily in your inner garden.

Love Thyself

You have made it this far in life. You're still standing and going at it every day. That *has* to count for something, right? I don't know if it came from my parents or what, but I'm extremely hard on myself. I constantly challenge myself and tell myself I can do much better. Don't do it the way I did; give yourself a pat on the back. Even though you cannot see the effects of such a practice, being hard on one's self can become a major energy drain. To keep a healthy balance, I now talk to myself in front of a mirror every morning to level my expectations for the day and to remind myself that whatever happens, I'm still proud of who I am. Affirmations is a great way to commit to your own success.

Sleep

There are a bunch of memes doing the rounds in the Internet depicting a typical bedroom super producer, working on music at night and then moving to the bed next to the desk to basically keep (mentally) producing/mixing while sleeping. In the words of Homer Simpson, "It's funny because it's true."

When you are a creative type, you cannot sleep until the mind has reached a satisfactory solution to an artistic problem. You will have to trick your mind into forgetting about the issue once your head touches the pillow. Create a strong sleep routine.

> *We are what we repeatedly do. Excellence, then, is not an act, but a habit.*
>
> —Aristotle

An ex-girlfriend of mine once explained to me how she did it. I mean the woman would literally close her eyes and fall asleep. I don't know about you, but that's a major slap in the face for people like me who twist and turn for hours before getting a couple of Zs. She said, "You need a sleep routine. Always go to bed and wake up at the same hour of the day." Now, I am *no* expert on the matter, but here are a few more tips:

1. Be smart about napping. It took me fifteen years to find the exact duration of my perfect midday nap.
2. Exercise more (get that calisthenics fire by my man Darrell).
3. Take a moment to clean your mind of creative shortcomings you might have had during the day before approaching the bedroom.
4. And the juggernaut: say no to TV, smartphones, and tablets in bed. Lately, I put myself on a program where I need to get one hour of no-screen time before bed—very, very difficult.

Relationships

Family. Lovers. Friendships. Business alliances. These are all integral parts of our happiness *as well as* our professional success.

I remember just before my divorce, I stayed all nights, all weekends, and all holidays caged in my home studio like a wild beast. If anyone had the audacity to call or, even worse, knock on the door, he or she would be greeted with a frown, a grunt, and maybe even the glare of sharp teeth ready to snap at unwelcome visitors.

All jokes aside, this woman I was married to gave me the single best piece of creative advice anyone ever gave me: when inspiration isn't there and frustration kicks in, it's time to unplug and spend quality time with friends, family, loved ones, or all of the above. Bouncing energy back and forth with real (ahem) human beings is crucial to our well-being and creativity. You never know when small talk will bring you your next great idea. I have heard a lot of producers talk about this, so it *must* be a major key.

Foster your relationships. Make time for important people. Stay on their radar.

Keep Learning

I will be eternally grateful to my parents for sending me to college and paying for everything. This has been a blessing both in the way I develop my reasoning and strategies and the way I present my ideas to the world. College gave me intellectual rigor as well as a structured work ethic.

In retrospect, though, I think I learned more in the ten years that followed college than in all of my academic career. You see, college does not teach you how to get the perfect job. It does not show you how to dream big, develop a vision, and establish the milestones you need to attain to fulfill that vision. So in that sense, I side with mentors like Tai Lopez and Gary Vaynerchuk: the most useful stuff to complete your hero journey (shout out to Joseph Campbell) will be learned by you at the school of hard knocks.

Business books. Self-help books. Audiobooks (if you're not the reading kind). YouTube tutorials. Online classes. Mentorships and personal development courses. We live in wonderful times. Access to information, for good and bad, has never been so quick and easy. Let's take advantage of it. Be like everybody else: when waiting in line at the grocery shop or between metro/bus stations, pull out that smartphone. But be different. Instead of looking aimlessly at your Facebook feed, read a few pages of a marketing book.

Here is my daily regimen:

- Thirty minutes of reading prior to work (usually self-help à la Tony Robbins)
- Thirty minutes of business reading at lunchtime (the latest Gary Vaynerchuk, for example)

- Thirty minutes to one hour of online mentoring in the evening (right now it's Mike Dillard's Self-made Man Society)
- Before bed, on my Apple TV, I'll usually watch two or three quick tutorials on sound design or mixing techniques.

Stay hungry. Quench that thirst for knowledge daily. In the words of Tai Lopez, give your brain a well-deserved six-pack.

Invest in Experiences, Not Things

The final pillar is a result of your hard work. You make great music. Making music brings joy. Music also brings money. Money should be used to bring in more joy.

In the words of Frank Lopez from *Scarface*, "Your biggest problem is not bringing in the stuff but what to do with all the fucking cash."

When I tell the story of how I quit a job as a manager for a Fortune 500 company to pursue a career in music, I always mention the fact that I had a six-figure income. Why? Not because I think it makes me look cool, or smart, or better than anyone else. You see, growing up, I came to see a six-figure income as a symbol of professional achievement. I always told myself, "Bro, the day you make a hundred grand is going to be the day you will have it made." Sure enough, that fateful day did come. I remember it as clear as day: *This is what 100K feels like?*

I felt betrayed. Money, a few clean suits, and a title didn't make me happier. It made it all the more obvious that money didn't buy happiness.

Well, then, what the fuck does?

I was so confident that being part of the corporate world would give me personal satisfaction and hopefully a little peace of mind. The destruction of these (mental) success symbols was, to this day, one of the greatest blessings in my life. Success was no longer an outside result. Success was the measure of my inner level of happiness. The need to compare myself and my accomplishments to others (finally) became irrelevant.

My younger brother had a tough life. He would probably tell you he never quite fit in with society's expectations. Like me, that pushed him to do a lot of soul-searching over the years. I am very proud to say that the kid gained a lot of insight and wisdom. He is a great teacher to me. When I told him money from the corporate gig didn't bring me any type of happiness, he replied, "I've been listening to this psychology podcast, and it seems research teams from fancy American colleges have come to realize that when it comes to money, happiness stems from investing in experiences, not things." Whoa.

So money *does* buy happiness. I knew it!

Here's the kicker: buying new toys makes us happy—for a short while. Buying experiences and the lasting memories they give may just last forever.

I see money as a vehicle. Happiness is about living to the fullest: tasting many different kinds of food, seeing nature in all its splendor, and indulging in cultural diversity. Money will take you there. You just have to answer this basic question: Where do you want to go?

Conclusion

Why, oh, why didn't i take the blue pill?
Let yourself see just how deep the rabbit hole goes

Now that the secret world of bedroom super producers has been unveiled before your eyes, there is no turning back. It is by far one of the most effective ways to create income with music online. Like I said a few times in this book, this method can create hourly rates similar to and even higher than what star producers earn. Yes, you can earn in the high six figures yearly. But more importantly, what happens once you start living this dream lifestyle? What will happen to you once you really start to be happy?

I often pinch myself to see if this is all really true. When I realize how fulfilling the past three years have been, I get very emotional. I never thought I deserved all of this. But that's just that loser talking again.

So I wrote this book to show my gratitude to the universe. This is my testament to this one universal truth: if you take that leap of faith to embark on your hero journey, you have no idea what life has in store for you. As synchronicity starts to kick in, you realize there is something really magical to this thing called life.

I also wrote this book to make it easier to explain to people what I do for a living. I always thought this would have a great ring to it at some fancy cocktail party: "I won't bore you with the specifics on such a wonderful night. Here…give me your e-mail address, and I'll make sure you get a copy of my book."

But what *did* we cover?

A Business Plan

Most people think it's about creating products and then finding people to buy them. The way of the bedroom super producer is to create a product that hordes of people are already searching for. Marketplaces are powerful allies and great teachers. Put your music out there and let the market help you become a better artist and a better business owner.

A Paradigm Shift

A lot of our colleagues will have to start thinking differently about selling their art. This is perfectly normal. The first step is to accept the change. The second step is to embrace it so that your creative business mind can take over and develop new streams of income every week.

Mental Tools

- To train our minds before embarking on the journey
- To stay focused on the path of the bedroom super producer
- To provide our brains with the best nourishment
- To become creative business people

Work Tools

- To work like the best
- To sound like the best
- To work faster than the best

A Proven Musical Approach

Great wisdom is usually found in one's heart. Music for media is not voodoo. It has a simple list of ingredients. Follow the recipe, work on your chops, give it your own unique spin, and things will fall into place. Keep it simple, stupid.

Marketing Tactics

It's not enough to put music out there. You have to do a bit of selling. No one can do it better. Understanding how content is found on the Internet through keyword strategies. Great copywriting is a skill you will use for the rest of your life.

Branding Tactics

Quality work is but one of the many aspects of presenting yourself in the best light possible. A bedroom super producer carries him- or herself above the pack in the digital arena. He or she looks sharper and more organized. He or she is easy to reach and quick to respond. He or she has a wealth of products and services to help businesses meet their content goals.

Multiple Streams of Income

Improving your methodology will help you create habits and products that can benefit your colleagues too. It will also free up a lot of time to develop other aspects of your business. Once you start working like a pro, you can start selling your production tools and get closer every day to financial freedom.

A Framework for Producer Happiness

I have been through mental and physical hell so some of my younger sisters and brothers don't have to. I have tried to touch the bottomless end of the self-destruction pool to no avail. There is no need for me to expose the grim details. Just take my word for it when I say that a bedroom super producer's success lies in a healthy, balanced lifestyle. Work hard on your well-being to play hard on your instruments.

Writing these last few words, I realize I'll have to read my own book at least once a year to remind myself why I'm here writing in the first place. LOL.

Finally, I wrote this book to give back to my community. There have never been so many kids with a music production dream. I remember how clueless I was when I started researching computer music. Finding good information was like looking for a needle in a haystack. You don't have to spend twenty years to sort it all out like I did. You can read this book and apply the concepts slowly but surely.

This is my way of making the world a better place. If knowledge is power, then I hope to empower the youth. I have been helped to become a bedroom super producer. I have helped peers become bedroom super producers. Now is the time to let the entire world know. In the words of Drake, thank me later.

More importantly, thank you. Your success is the brother- and sisterhood's success.

Printed in Poland
by Amazon Fulfillment
Poland Sp. z o.o., Wrocław